Conquer Your Concentration

First Printed in Great Britain by
Obex Publishing Ltd in 2020

2 4 6 8 10 9 7 5 3 1

Copyright Jean-Claude Leveque, 2020

Jean-Claude Leveque has asserted his right under the Copyright, Designs and Patents Act 1988 to be identified as the author of this work.

All rights reserved. No parts of this publication may be reproduced, stored in a retrieval system, or transmitted in any form or by any means, electronic, mechanical, photocopying, recording or otherwise, without the prior permission of the copyright owner.

Paperback ISBN	978-1-913454-11-1
eBook ISBN	978-1-913454-12-8

A CIP catalogue record for this book is available from the British Library.

Obex Publishing Ltd.
Reg. No. 12169917

*"Lack of direction, not lack of time, is the problem.
We all have twenty-four hour days."*
Zig Ziglar

CONTENTS

INTRODUCTION 6

CHAPTER 1: WHAT IS FOCUS? 10
    Is Focus And Concentration The Same Thing?............................. 11
    Three Different Types of Focus 12
    How Does Focus Increase Productivity? 17
    Points to Remember From This Chapter 19

CHAPTER 2: DO YOU HAVE A VISION?.......................... 21
    Why Should You Have a Vision? 22
    How to Use Visualisation to Picture What You Really Want 24
    Why is Clarity of Mind Important? 27
    How to Make Your Vision More Exciting, And Therefore More Motivating... 29
    Points to Remember From This Chapter 30

CHAPTER 3: WHAT IS YOUR 'WHY'? 32
    Why is 'Why' so Important? 33
    How to Give Your Visions Meaning............................... 35
    How to Increase Your Motivation 36
    Points to Remember From This Chapter 38

CHAPTER 4: THE ART OF UNSHAKEABLE FOCUS 39
    Understanding What Is Important And What Isn't..................... 40
    Do You Have Your Head Turned Easily? 43
    Learning to do More With Less...................................... 46
    Keeping Your Eyes on The Prize..................................... 48
    Points to Remember From This Chapter 50

CHAPTER 5: THE BIG TWO - PRIORITISING AND SCHEDULING 51
    How to Approach a Task in The Best Way 53
    How to Prioritise Effectively 57
    When Your Day Doesn't Go According to Plan 62

WHAT IS SCHEDULING? 65
POINTS TO REMEMBER FROM THIS CHAPTER 69

CHAPTER 6: YOUR NUMBER ONE ENEMY - PROCRASTINATION ...71

WHAT IS PROCRASTINATION? 73
5 WAYS TO AVOID PROCRASTINATION 76
LEARNING THAT PERFECTIONISM ISN'T REAL 85
POINTS TO REMEMBER FROM THIS CHAPTER 87

CHAPTER 7: IS YOUR LIFESTYLE AFFECTING YOUR FOCUS? 89

TOP FOODS FOR FOCUS 90
WHY EXERCISE IS IMPORTANT 94
SLEEP, GLORIOUS SLEEP! 96
A WORD ABOUT MENTAL HEALTH 99
POINTS TO REMEMBER FROM THIS CHAPTER 103

CHAPTER 8: IMPROVE YOUR FOCUS TODAY! 105

11 STRATEGIES TO NATURALLY INCREASE YOUR FOCUS 107
TRY A DIGITAL DETOX 108
IDENTIFY AND CUT OUT REGULAR DISTRACTIONS................................. 113
LEARN TO INVEST IN YOURSELF.. 119
FIND A NEW HOBBY AND WORK TO BE THE BEST YOU CAN 121
IDENTIFY WHAT IS IMPORTANT TO YOU... 124
REMEMBER THAT BREAKS ARE IMPORTANT 128
TRY MINDFULNESS MEDITATION 131
SET SMALL GOALS ON A DAILY BASIS... 136
CHANGE YOUR ENVIRONMENT.. 139
AVOID MULTI-TASKING AT ALL COSTS 145
USE BRAIN TRAINING EXERCISES.. 147
POINTS TO TAKE FROM THIS CHAPTER 150

CONCLUSION 152

Introduction

Are you focused?

Let's rephrase that to make it easier to answer - do you consider yourself able to focus no matter what the circumstances?

Do you even know what focused actually means? Many people don't!

If you want to be productive in life, if you want to achieve, get more done with the time you have and actually get somewhere, you need focus. It's like the magic ingredient in the recipe to revolutionise your life.

The problem is, we have a million and one distractions coming our way every single day, and we're more connected than we've ever been. Our phones connect us to not only those close to us in our lives but the entire world too. Anyone can find you via social media and most of us keep our feeds open on our phones, so we're within easy reach of absolutely anyone, whether we know them or not!

In addition, we have the world at our fingertips and as much information available as we can consume in a day. You might think that's a good thing and sure, in some ways it is, but if you're constantly switched on, how are you supposed to focus and concentrate on anything clearly?

This is such a thing as information overload and most of us experience it every single day!

If you find it hard to focus, or if you simply want to know a few techniques that will help you block out the white noise and deal with what's in front of you, this book is for you.

We are going to help you increase your capacity to focus. We're going to do that by showing you exactly what focus is, telling you what doesn't help it, what does, and how to use those positive techniques in a healthy and productive way.

By the end of this book, you'll not only be very sure what focus is, but you'll be so laser-sharp focused that you're ticking off your to-do list before the end of the day is even near!

Sounds good, right?

You see, the thing is, if you don't have focus then you don't have determination, you don't have the motivation, and you won't achieve anything. It might sound harsh, but it's the truth. You need focus to be able to make it through difficult times, to be able to overcome hurdles and problems that stand in your way, and you need it to be able to spot potential road blocks before they even become an issue in the first place.

Put simply, focus is your friend and it leads you into a merry band of other very useful friends too, namely concentration, productivity, success, achievement, the list goes on.

So, you might think that there are more attractive subjects to learn about, perhaps how to make the most of the time you have in the day with time management methods, how to achieve your dreams, and how to increase your daily motivation, but do you know what sits at the heart of all those so-called interesting subjects?

You guessed it - focus.

Nothing gets done unless you pay attention to it, at least nothing gets done well at least. Being a productive person increases your confidence, gives you a greater sense of self worth and allows you to reach your deeper goals in life. Without the ability to focus, it could very well be that everything falls apart over time.

This isn't something you should be aiming for! This book is going to change the horizon for you if you're someone who struggles with focus. You're going to learn how to set the groundwork, feed your brain what it needs, and you're going to learn how to harness the power of different strategies, which will get you where you need to be.

It takes time, effort, and a willingness to commit to the process, but it's something that can be done, no matter what your starting point.

So, enough with the procrastinating, let's get started on your journey towards total focus right now.

Chapter 1:
What is Focus?

We've mentioned the F word several times (no, not that one), but what exactly does it mean?

We can't write a book about focus if we don't give it a meaning and a firm definition at the start.

The thing is if you look 'focus' up in the dictionary, it will come up with several definitions according to situations. For us, however, focus means to pay close attention.

That's probably the best way to define it.

That doesn't just mean concentrating for a short while, it means thinking ahead, anticipating problems, thinking back over your past experiences and trying to work out whether you can use those to help you side-step common problems. Focus means total concentration, not only on what you have in front of you but also on anything which might become an issue and threaten your progress and success.

In this chapter, we're going to cover the basics, and one question which many people ask is this - are focus and concentration the same thing?

Is Focus And Concentration The Same Thing?

The answer is no, not really, but they are extremely closely linked to the point where the two terms are often used interchangeably.

You need to focus in order to concentrate. You can't concentrate without learning to focus first.

The reason is because of those small differences.

We've already mentioned that focus means to pay attention to something, but concentrating is more about the depth of focus, i.e. paying even closer attention and looking for very small details within a smaller area.

For instance, you'll hear the word 'concentrated' when buying orange squash, as just one example. In this case, there is more orange in a smaller amount of juice, so you don't need to use as much. The concentration is focused on a smaller area.

In work terms, when you concentrate, your attention is greater in terms of depth.

You cannot focus your attention on those smaller areas unless you focus, because otherwise, you wouldn't be paying any attention.

Does that answer your question?

The good news is that one affects the other. If you focus more, you concentrate better. If you concentrate better, your focus increases even more. They're not the same in terms of definition, but they're very useful when used hand in hand.

For the purposes of this book, we're trying to increase focus in order to help you do more in a shorter space of time and therefore work towards your goals and achieve your dreams. You need to be able to focus in order to pay attention to those goals and dreams, and as a result, your concentration on each step of the way will be greater.

That equals success.

Three Different Types of Focus

Whilst researchers are still trying to work out the inner dealings of the brain and how the anatomy works together in order to keep us ticking along nicely, they mostly agree that there are three main types of focus. That doesn't mean another won't be discovered any time soon, however! The brain is a complex organ that continually surprises us with its capacity for wonderment.

For now, however, there are thought to be three main types of focus. In order to learn how to increase your focus, you need to understand these types and work out which areas you might need to work a little harder on.

These types are:

- Inner focus
- Outer focus
- Other focus

Inner focus is about your thoughts and feelings, basically anything inside of your own mind. By learning to increase your inner focus you can understand your emotions better, learn to control negative emotions and subsequent reactions, whilst also learning to listen to your intuition and trust what it is telling you. By developing your inner focus you can also learn to make better, stronger decisions.

Learning to increase the capacity of your inner focus takes some inward thinking. This means perhaps looking towards meditation, becoming more mindful and learning to live in the present day and not stuck in the past or living in fear of the future, and it is also about learning to understand your own emotional triggers and how to control them. This type of practice certainly takes time but it's very beneficial.

On the other hand, the external focus is about what is going on around us and the forces and influences which are going on in the outside world. In a business or work-sense, this would be the management or leadership you have, or in a general sense, it could be the situations that are happening in your personal life which you don't have direct control of. These are elements that can affect our focus and as a result, our concentration.

You can increase your external focus by arming yourself with knowledge and learning to understand what is going on around you. For instance, you may be able to increase your external focus by learning about the economic situation around you at work or learning more about the background to problems that are happening in your life. You can do this by reading upon specific subjects, or by having a mentor in your life, connected to the problem or situation at hand.

Finally, we have other focus.

Other focus is about other people around us and how well equipped you are to pay attention to them completely. This can be reading their body language, picking up on non-verbal cues, your listening skills (the ability to really listen and not just hear words), and also how able you are to keep your mind in the moment and stop it wandering off on a tangent.

Developing your other focus is another inward route. You need to be more mindful of the people around you and develop the perception to see when they may be feeling something but not telling you. Again, this is best done via body language cues.

You could also ask for feedback on whether or not the people around you are actually going through what you think they are. This will help you to figure out whether your social awareness and perception is right, or a little off the mark.

Despite these three main types of focus which researchers present us with, there are two other types which you might find useful to learn about. These stimulus-driven and voluntary-focus.

These types are less about perception and more about what is going on around us.

- **Voluntary-focus, also known as top-down focus** - This type of focus kicks into hyperdrive when you're trying to reach something, so perhaps if you're studying for an exam or you're trying to get a promotion at work. It is when you are focused on achieving a specific goal and helps you to see past the moment and towards the bigger picture.

- **Stimulus-driven focus, also known as bottom-up focus** - On the other hand, bottom-up focus is driven by your immediate external environment, e.g. the noises you hear. This links to the body's fight or flight stress response, e.g. a very loud noise will cause you to jump and hyper-focus on your environment to try and figure out what it is. In that case, you have no choice but to focus on investigating that noise and everything else you were trying to focus on drifts away.

Learning to be less stimulus-driven and more voluntary-focus takes a little time and requires you to develop overall focus first of all. As you work through the strategies we're going to cover late in the book, you'll find that your loud noises and other external stimuli will become less troublesome to you and won't cause your focus to steer off target quite so easily as a result.

How Does Focus Increase Productivity?

It might sound like an obvious question, but how exactly does the ability to focus more effectively increase your daily productivity?

It comes down to several things:

- Making fewer mistakes
- Building your confidence
- The ability to do more in the time you have, e.g. time management
- Decreasing stress
- Looking beyond the obvious by increasing close concentration skills

When you learn how to focus more effectively, you're less distracted by anything going on in your immediate environment. Sure, your phone might be beeping left, right and centre with social media updates and you're probably still going to be tempted to check them, but you'll find it easier not to. As a result, you're less stimulus-driven and more able to pay attention to the task at hand. This means fewer mistakes and a greater level of quality to your work.

By learning how to focus you'll also use time management techniques as part of the process. This will enable you to work smarter, therefore getting more done in the time you have. As a result, you're less stressed out, because you're not constantly chasing your tail and trying to finish four tasks in the time that only realistically allows for two to be completed, and you feel more confident as a result because you're the one in control of your workload.

Of course, we mentioned earlier that learning to focus also helps to increase your ability to concentrate, so by increasing your focus quality, you're able to look beyond the obvious and see things in greater detail. Again, this boosts the quality of your work and reduces the chances of making needless mistakes.

All of the above increases productivity and helps you become more effective at work, in your home life, and in achieving your life's goals.

When you look at it that way, there's really no downside in putting in the work to increase your ability to focus!

Points to Remember From This Chapter

This first chapter is designed to help you understand what focus actually is. Only when you know what something really is can you work to increase the amount of it that you have. The same goes for focus.

By now, you should understand that focus is to pay attention and that it is slightly different from concentration. Despite that, extra focus increases concentration and vice versa.

There are several different types of focus and the story is a little more complex than you might have thought at first. In order to improve your focus you need to increase your overall awareness, both inside, outside, and also on other people.

The main points to take from this chapter are:

- Focus is defined as 'the ability to pay attention'
- Whilst focus and concentration are often used as interchangeable terms, they're not the same. However, one does increase the other
- The three main types of focus are inner focus, outer focus and other focus
- There is also voluntary focus (top down focus) and stimulus driven focus (bottom up focus)

- Becoming more focused can make you a more productive person.

Chapter 2:
Do You Have a Vision?

The ability to live a healthy and happy life relies upon many things, but it also involves the use of imagination.

Without imagination, we're unable to think of goals we might want to achieve in the future, or the life we want to work towards for ourselves. This is also known as our 'vision'.

If you ask Wikipedia, it will tell you that vision is "the ability to think about or plan the future with imagination or wisdom". As you can see, you need to be able to think creatively and use your imagination to think about your future, but you also need to use your wisdom to know what is and isn't possible.

Of course, with hard work most things are possible, but not everything. For instance, dreaming of becoming a prince or princess is more likely to be literally that - a dream, and not a vision. We do need a pinch of common sense and to rein in our most 'out there' dreams but if your dream can become a goal, then you will have a vision in order to achieve it.

So, how does this link in with focus?

In order to achieve any goal, i.e. a vision, you need focus. You need to pay attention to the step by step tasks you have to go through in order to reach that overall goal, and the more focus you have, the more concentration you'll have. As a result, your approach will be more goal-oriented and far less likely to be driven off course by the smallest distraction.

Why Should You Have a Vision?

Surely life is more interesting and worthwhile when you have something to work towards?

If you have a picture in your mind of what you want your life to look like, or a goal you really want to achieve, the motivation to reach that aim will enrich your life in many different ways.

For instance, perhaps you want to study towards a degree and then look for work as a teacher. This is your dream and the thing you want the most in your life. In essence, becoming a teacher in the future is your vision, but studying to obtain a degree is the work you need to complete in order to get there - that is your immediate focus.

Without the focus, your vision is impossible – because, without the degree, you cannot become a teacher.

When you reach your future aim, you will feel full of pride and fulfilment. You will be proud of what you have achieved and you'll feel confident, with a higher degree of self worth. From there, you learn that with hard work, you can reach towards your greatest dreams, and it will probably spur you on to try and hit another milestone in your life.

A vision helps give us something to work towards, something to aim towards, and that helps to add meaning and depth to life. Without that, what do you have? Sure, you have your health, your family and your friends, but otherwise, you will simply tick through life, not really achieving much and never really having those highs and lows that are part and parcel of a well-lived life.

Vision is motivation in its purest form. It's a visualisation of the life you really want for yourself.

How to Use Visualisation to Picture What You Really Want

Now we know what a vision is and why it's important, how do you get one?

By dreaming, that's how!

This is the fun part. This is when you let your imagination run wild and imagine all manner of wonderful things you want for yourself. Of course, you might need to rein yourself in occasionally, when you start dreaming about stately homes and knighthoods but provided your goals are within reach with plenty of hard work, there's no reason why you can't put a plan together and start making slow and steady progress towards achieving them.

A vision is obtained by visualisation.

This basically means that you picture your life when you have achieved the thing you want the most. You'll explore how it really feels, what it looks like, what it smells like, what it tastes like, and every other piece of sensory information you can get your hands (and senses) on. How do you do this?

By using your imagination and letting it go to places you might never have allowed it to go before.

In order to obtain a vision via visualisation, you need to have an idea of what you really want. You might not know the specifics, but you know the end goal. For instance, you might want to own your home, or you might want to go backpacking around the world. You might want to obtain a promotion in your current role, or you might want to retrain completely and head off around the world.

In order to visualise, you need to focus.

There's that word again!

Learning to shut out the noise around us isn't easy, and the first time you do it you'll probably notice that you struggle. This might even extend into the first few times you do it, but stick with it. You will get there in the end.

Try this.

- Sit somewhere quietly, or lay down if you prefer to
- Make sure you're not going to be disturbed and turn off your phone
- Anything which is irritating you, such as tight clothing, sunlight coming in through the window etc, get rid of it in order to be completely comfortable. You can't let your mind wander and visualise your end goal if you're distracted by something external

- When you're ready, picture the thing you want the most in your mind
- Try and pull as many details into it as possible, such as what it looks like visually, what it feels like emotionally, the people around you in the vision, what they're doing, whether they're happy or not.
- Stick with it and imagine as many details as you can
- As you're doing this, do a quick scan of your emotions and see how you feel about it all; do you feel happy? Sad? Accomplished? Proud?
- Stay in the vision for as long as you feel comfortable, but the moment you start to notice your attention wavering, call it quits for the day. This is something you'll need to revisit several times, in order to build up the full visualisation.

The more you attempt to visualise your goal, the easier it will become and the more details you'll be able to pull into it. When you've gone as far as you can with it, you've completed your vision. This is something you can use to motivate you whenever your focus is starting to dwindle, but by using the strategies we're going to talk more about as we move through the book, you'll find that happens less and less, enabling your vision and motivation to grow stronger.

Why is Clarity of Mind Important?

Achieving anything in life requires determination, but it also requires a clear mind.

You can't focus if your mind is constantly cluttered with thoughts and the rest of your day's to-do list. Being able to declutter and clear your mind is therefore vital if you want to be able to focus, concentrate and then work towards the things you want and need in life.

As you will have noticed when you attempted to visualise for the first time, things enter into your mind subconsciously and can lead your thoughts off on a tangent. It is these types of situations you need to try and get a handle on if you want to be able to increase your focus. By doing this, you'll also notice that you can reflect back on your day and other aspects of your life far easier, and you'll be able to think much more deeply as a result.

So, how can you achieve greater clarity of mind?

- **Meditation** - Guided meditation is ideal for first-timers, as it gives you something to place your concentrate on whilst also trying to dull out the noise around you. You may need to practice a few times in order to get to the quietest space possible but stick with it. Meditation has plenty of benefits

and by doing your best to obtain them, you'll also notice that your clarity of mind, and therefore your focus, is greater.
- **Spending time alone** - Some people are terrified at the idea of spending time alone, but it's actually extremely beneficial! Take yourself off somewhere quiet, perhaps to the beach, on a walk through the forest, or to a clifftop and sit and think. Reflect and allow your mind to quieten. When you're not surrounded by quite so much of the regular noise that comes with general life, it's easier to declutter your mind.
- **Learn to accept life as it is** - We're always striving for something, and whilst aiming for goals is never a bad thing, if you're always attempting to reach something, you don't have the time to really sit and take in what is around you right now. As a result, you're missing out on life! Learn to accept life as it is right now and see how freeing that feels, and how content you're likely to feel as a result.
- **Cut out the unnecessary stuff** - Focus your goals to the most concentrated aspect possible. Find out what you need and what you want right now. Then, turn the microscope onto that, to find out what you need to do to achieve it. Cutting out the unnecessary will help you to declutter and focus far more easily, also giving you greater clarity of mind in the process.

How to Make Your Vision More Exciting, And Therefore More Motivating

In order to really motivate yourself to move towards your goals, therefore increasing your focus and concentration, you need to find a way to make your visions exciting. That means adding as much detail as you possibly can.

If you think about when you're actually excited about something, you imagine it, right? This means you try and figure out in your mind what it's going to feel like, what it's going to look like and how it's going to affect you. This helps to build up the excitement and therefore pushes you towards making it a reality. The same goes for any type of goal you have.

Find a point in that goal that really excites you and as a result, you'll find that having a vision and being able to visualise the smaller details will come to you much easier. When you can experience something before you've actually achieved it, it gives you a window into how it's going to feel. That is often enough to motivate you onwards.

So, add as much colour and detail to your visualisations as you can. Really delve deeply and focus on the positive aspects. By doing this, you're motivating yourself further.

Points to Remember From This Chapter

In this chapter, we have talked about the importance of having a vision. You cannot improve your focus if you have no idea what you're trying to achieve! You can create your vision via your imagination; something most of us fail to use to its optimum potential!

By tapping into your imagination you're able to explore what you really want in life. By doing that, you can then imagine it in greater detail, pushing you towards actually doing the work and getting what you want.

The main points to remember from this chapter are:

- Your imagination is vital if you want to be able to achieve your greatest goals in life
- Having a vision is important because it gives you direction and encourages motivation
- Visualisation will help you to tap into your imagination and give you the motivation to push forward and achieve the things you want, by giving you a heads up on how it's going to feel when you achieve it

- Clarity of mind is important if you want to improve your overall focus
- Being able to clear your mind of clutter can be difficult at first, but heading out into nature alone is a good place to start
- Adding colour and detail to your vision can help to motivate you further.

Chapter 3:
What is Your 'Why'?

In order to push yourself to do something and pay attention to the smaller details, i.e. focus, you need to know exactly why you're doing it.

You get up and go to work in the morning because you need the money. You go and see your parents because you want to see them and enjoy your time. You go to the supermarket to buy groceries because you need to eat.

You have a 'why' for almost everything and the things you don't have a 'why' for, you probably don't end up doing at all.

This chapter is going to talk about why it's important to have a 'why', and how to make your visions as meaningful as possible, by using that 'why' as power. In our last chapter, we talked about the need for a vision and how to visualise. We mentioned that by adding details to your visions you can motivate yourself via excitement. Now we're going to talk about how you can increase your focus on a specific goal by giving it a true meaning.

Remember, everything we talk about in this book will increase your focus in the end. We might talk about motivation and you might end up wondering how that's got much to do with paying attention and focusing, but look at this way - without motivation, you're not going to be bothered about focusing on anything and therefore you won't achieve it.

Having a 'why' does the same thing. You're motivating yourself and pushing yourself to want to do something enough to put the extra energy and time into the cause. By doing that, you're naturally increasing your focus.

Why is 'Why' so Important?

So why exactly do you need a 'why'?

Humans are a pretty lazy species. Yes, us, you, everyone else, we're all pretty lazy. Unless we have a reason to do something, we don't tend to do it. When you think about it, why would you? Having a reason gives you instant motivation.

For instance, you might start to go swimming in the mornings before work because you want to become fitter and leaner because you're about to go on holiday. Otherwise, you wouldn't be bothered about getting up early and going swimming!

Having a 'why' gives you a push and therefore naturally increases your focus. Without a 'why' you simply don't do it and don't even think to do it. You might consider it for a second, but it will remain nothing more than a dream.

If there is something you want in life or a task you really want to complete, identify your 'why'. What is your reason?

Why do you want this thing? What is it going to do for you? Simplify it down into a why and stick with it. Use this as your primary motivation.

Of course, you might not be able to simplify it down into just one reason why. In that case, to avoid complicating matters, look for the most important reason why. If you need to write it down to remind you of how important it is, do so. Many people use positive affirmations in this way, so there's no reason why you can't use your reason why in the same way. If it serves to push your motivation, go for it!

How to Give Your Visions Meaning

Having a 'why' will give your visions a true meaning because they will show you the reason behind your desire to achieve whatever it is you're pushing towards. Again, having a 'why' means that you won't give in and that there's a reason greater than anything else to keep going.

The best way to give your vision a true meaning is to sit down and really think about what it means to you. If you don't achieve this, how will you feel? Will it detrimentally affect your life? Will you have regrets? Giving your vision a meaning is about understanding it's real meaning to you and then working towards ensuring that you don't end up experiencing the negatives of not actually getting there.

In reality, a vision is a mental picture, but in order to make it mean something more, it needs to have feelings attached to it. In our last chapter, we talked about visualisation and by focusing on this aspect you can actually experience the feelings you would have if you achieved it, or didn't. That is another high-quality way to attach a meaning to a vision.

How to Increase Your Motivation

In order to be focused, you need to be motivated, and vice versa. So, how can you naturally increase your motivation and therefore help your focus on its way too?

- **Set small goals that can be measured** - It's very easy to start procrastinating on a task that looks too large to achieve. For instance, if you're trying to reach the end of a life goal, it's going to take many years to get there in some cases. When you look at the job as a whole, it's off-putting because it's so huge. However, if you break it down into smaller, bite-sized chunks, you can make small amounts of progress, which you can measure along the way. With each chunk you achieve, celebrate the achievement of a small goal.
- **Create a personal mantra** - Positive affirmations are not just for trying to become a more positive person, they can also be used to increase your motivation towards achieving something. Look for a mantra that suits you, or make up your own. Something like "I will not give in, I am strong and I am able". It can be anything! Repeat it whenever you feel like your motivation is wavering.
- **Make your goal known** - There is no better motivator than telling people what you're trying to do. This means you're not going to give up easily because you're scared of people thinking

you've failed! You could say it's a negative way to motivate yourself, but it's a very effective one you can try. So, tell people what you're trying to do and give them regular check-ins on your progress. The likelihood is that they'll keep asking you how you're doing and you won't want to tell them that you've not done anything about your goal for a while! You could also write a blog or document your journey on social media.

- **Stick to a routine** - Create a routine that allows you to make slow and steady progress, whilst also having time for things you enjoy. This means you're less likely to rebel against whatever is taking up so much of your time and you'll stick to the goals you're setting for yourself. This motivates you to continue on because you can see the progress you're making.
- **Visualise your end goal** - We've mentioned this a few times already, but it works for motivation too. Make sure you spend some time visualising what your end goal looks like and feels like. Remember to add the 'why' to your vision and you'll feel it on a deeper level.

Points to Remember From This Chapter

In this chapter, we have focused on having a 'why' for the things you do in life. When you know why you're doing something, it's easier to stay on track and therefore, easier to focus too. Having a 'why' means you have a source of motivation and when you tap into that why and really push yourself to imagine how it's going to be once the goal is complete, you'll find it far easier to actually achieve the things you want in life.

The main points to take from this chapter are:

- Having a 'why' is a reason want to do something
- Attaching a why gives you motivation and forces you to reach for the end result
- You are more likely to focus closely if you really want your reason why
- Motivation is easier to find if you break your goals down into easier to achieve chunks
- Having a routine which is easy to manage is also a good way to achieve motivation
- You will find your motivation and focus naturally increases when you make your goals public - you will not want to fail or be perceived to fail by the people around you.

Chapter 4:
The Art of Unshakeable Focus

If you want to succeed at anything in life, you need to be focused. That's something we've already ascertained.

The fact you're reading this book shows us that you want to develop the type of focus that is not going to be shaken or wavered by outside influences, and the type of focus which you can rely upon to help you through hard times and still achieve the things you really want in life.

Of course, as with anything in life, developing focus to that degree times time and effort.

Despite that, it can be done!

First things first, what exactly is unshakeable focus?

Basically, there are a million and one things that could come to throw you off track. You might end up procrastinating because you're tired and the task you need to do simply isn't as fun as watching TV. You might be feeling generally unmotivated for no specific reason and as a result, the task you're supposed to do, the one task that is going to help you move towards your final goal, goes by the wayside.

When you're not focused it's very easy to become distracted and as a result, you let your goals and your dreams pass you by.

In order to be focused you need to be completely committed. Without that, you have literally nothing. You need to commit to the task at hand without any doubt, and you need to know your 'why' as we mentioned in our last chapter. When you have those two things, you're almost halfway to achieving unshakeable focus, with a few extras to ensure you don't end up being thrown off course at the last minute.

Understanding What Is Important And What Isn't

In order to develop that unshakeable focus you need to achieve your aims in life, you need to be able to cut out the background noise and focus on what is important. There are many things in life that come our way that we really don't need to pay attention to. As a result, we focus on the wrong things, derailing our efforts to reach our aims and goals. Big mistake.

So, how are you supposed to know what is important versus what really isn't?

By knowing what you want.

For instance, if you know that you want to save up enough money to buy your first car, you know that you need to cut out some unnecessary expenditures and work towards creating a savings plan. Certain things may come your way which tempt you and cause you to spend some of your hard-earned savings, therefore setting your original plan back a few steps.

When you look at that example you can see what matters and what doesn't.

The thing you want to save for matters, e.g. the car. The things that don't matter are the temptations that come your way that throw you off track.

However, it's easy to see that in retrospect. In the moment, when perhaps your focus isn't quite as unshakeable as it should be, you've somehow lost some of your motivation and maybe you're feeling a little down and in need of a pick me up, it's very easy to think "ah, just do it" and you spend some of that cash on a treat to make you feel better in the moment. Of course, the guilt comes later when you wish you hadn't bothered.

For this reason too, it's important to make sure that you don't create unrealistic goals. You cannot save every single penny you make; you need to have the occasional treat from time to time and look forward to things too.

Understanding the important things versus the non-important things will help you to maintain your focus, perhaps when times get a little rough.

So, what is important to you?

What are you trying to achieve?

Once you've answered that question, attach your 'why' to it. By doing that, you're halfway towards achieving unshakeable focus. Next, you need to try a little brain training to help keep your mind on the things that matter and avoid it being distracted by the unnecessary things instead.

Whenever something threatens to rob you of your focus, acknowledge it and ask whether or not it is important. If it is, by all means, go with it; if it's not, let it go.

Do You Have Your Head Turned Easily?

Are you easily distracted?

We've mentioned temptations a little already, but are you someone who can easily be distracted into doing something other than the task they have in front of them? Do you procrastinate with ease?

Learning to adopt a full-blown focus to everything you do takes time, but it can be done. Try this deep focus exercise.

- Choose one task to complete
- Adopt 100% of your time, attention and focus to that task for a full 30 seconds
- Whenever anything else tries to enter into your mind, push it away and lock your focus down onto that task. Do not allow your mind to wander
- Once 30 seconds are over, give yourself a short break of a few minutes and then repeat the process.

It sounds easy, but 30 seconds is a long time when your brain is battling against you and desperately wants to do something else! The more you do this exercise, the easier it will get and you'll find it easier to totally focus on a task without thinking of anything else.

The reason this exercise is so difficult is that we're bombarded with sensory information every single second of every day. We're constantly thinking, jumping from subject to subject, always connected, always switched on; as a result, it's very difficult to keep your mind focused on just one thing.

For that reason, keep practising this particular method over the course of a month. Do it daily and record your progress. At the end of the month, look at your starting point compared to where you are at the end.

Can you see a difference?

It's likely that you will, but at the time it might not feel like much is happening. Focus is a muscle that needs to have a good workout on a regular basis. You need to strengthen it so that when you call upon it in action, it's flexible, stronger, and works every time.

A little later we're going to talk at length about procrastination, which is an extremely easy trap to fall into. However, being distracted by everything around you is something you can control if you learn to keep strengthening that focus muscle and keep your attention where it needs to be.

Some people use delayed gratification as a way to keep their attention on the task at hand. This might work for you, so it's something you might like to try as a trial. Put simply, you promise yourself a reward if you finally get to the end of a specific task.

For instance, if you need to finish a report at work and it's so unbelievably boring that you would rather be doing anything else instead, you might find it easy to tell yourself that you can do it tomorrow. That's procrastination. If that report is part of your end goal, e.g. its a step on the way to completing your biggest goal in life, you're basically damaging your efforts before you've even started.

So, tell yourself that if you complete the report that day, you'll allow yourself a takeaway for dinner that night, you're giving yourself a reason to work, something to aim towards, and motivation to keep going. If you achieve completion of that report, have the takeaway. If you don't, you don't get it.

Try it for yourself and see if you find it a useful way to avoid having your head turned by everything around you. You'll also find that the stronger your natural ability to focus becomes, the more able you'll be to complete tasks that don't seem all that attractive or exciting to you.

Learning to do More With Less

Have you heard of minimalism?

This is basically putting the focus back on experiences and living in the moment and avoiding the need to purchase material items for happiness. It's also about streamlining your working processes and your entire environment, in order to help you think more clearly.

By learning to do more with less, you'll find that your focus is sharper as a result.

Let's explain why.

Have you ever tried to concentrate in a messy space? Perhaps you sit at someone else's desk at work for the day and you're surrounded by their sticky notes, their unfinished work and everything else they keep on their work surface. Sure, you have a small space to do your own work but everything around you can seem like it's closing in on you. As a result, you can't focus as well as you otherwise would be able to, and you end up procrastinating because you're annoyed with yourself for not being able to focus.

The same can be said for your general living environment. If your house is cluttered and full of mess, you're going to feel mentally bogged down.

This isn't going to help you focus on anything other than the mess around you.

Some people say that a messy desk is the sign of a creative mind, but it's more likely to be the sign of someone quite unfocused and unproductive.

To see what your personal mess level is, try working at a messy desk or generally messy environment for a week and then switch it up to something tidy. Where do you get the best results?

It's likely that you'll see your best results from a tidy environment.

This is partly what minimalism teaches us, but it's also about helping us to notice the thing that are really important in life, versus the things we just think are important.

If you remember, we mentioned the ability to recognise the important things at the start of this chapter. Decluttering your space and therefore decluttering your mind could help you with that very endeavour.

In terms of focus, a streamlined approach, therefore teaching you how to achieve more with less, will help you to avoid distractions and keep your eyes firmly where they're supposed to be.

Try it for yourself - get rid of anything in your immediate space that you really don't need. This is a good opportunity to gift things to those less fortunate, send items you don't want to a charity shop, or if you really want to, sell a few items for some extra cash. By doing this, you'll notice that you feel lighter almost immediately. Try and avoid cramming everything into a cupboard where you can't see it, as that's only going to continue weighing heavy on your mind - you know it's in there still!

Commit to decluttering on all levels and see how good you feel afterwards. The chances are that by doing this, you'll contribute to your overall focus level, and by using the other advice and suggestions we're talking about throughout this book, you'll notice small changes in your ability level.

Keeping Your Eyes on The Prize

Let's just give a quick nod back to the 'why' side of things and overall motivation. Without motivation, you're literally wasting your time. You need to find a personal way to keep your eyes on the prize so that you're able to work towards your goals at a slow yet steady rate.

So, what is your 'why' and how are you reminding yourself of it on a daily basis? Are you writing it down, as we suggested earlier? Have you created your own mantra or positive affirmation, to help you to keep moving when you seem to be stuck?

There are going to be problems that come your way throughout life which threaten to derail whatever it is you're trying to achieve at the time. Perhaps you're not actually trying to achieve anything per se, but you're working towards bettering yourself self-esteem and how you feel about yourself generally. As these hurdles approach, we have to learn how to jump over them with ease, and your focus and motivation to do that will be stronger if you can keep your eyes firmly on the thing you want the most.

Perhaps your aim isn't to achieve something you can see or touch, perhaps it's something you can only feel; maybe you want to learn to become more self-assured and confident within yourself. That's never a bad aim to reach for!

This type of self-development aim is always going to have hurdles and roadblocks to find your way over and through, and the single best way to avoid them becoming massive barriers on your way to progress is to keep your eyes firmly on the thing you want the most. Reassure yourself, be kind to yourself, give yourself a break when you need one, and understand that whilst life is always going to attempt to trip us up occasionally, that doesn't mean we need to allow it to derail us completely.

By understanding this on a deeper level, you'll maintain your focus, your concentration, and your motivation, whilst probably improving all three at the same time.

Points to Remember From This Chapter

- It's important to realise that life will always try to throw us curveballs and we need to be prepared for these by keeping our eyes firmly on the thing we want the most, or what we're trying to achieve
- If you find procrastination and general distractions to be a major problem, trying a deep focusing exercise and building up the amount of time you spend doing it, will help you overcome the temptation
- Learning to do more with less can help you build a greater sense of achievement and can also help you avoid distractions
- Decluttering your living, working and mental spaces can help you to focus far more effectively.

Chapter 5:
The Big Two - Prioritising And Scheduling

Up to now, we've talked about the mental attitude you need to have when learning how to increase your natural focus, motivation and how to overcome problems with decluttering and a positive attitude. However, specific strategies can also be a huge help.

The ability to focus doesn't come easily to everyone, and whilst you might feel like you can focus to a certain extent, being able to do this for long periods of time, and completely, can be very difficult indeed. However, by organising your time more effectively and learning to focus on the important things first of all, you'll give yourself a much better shot at your main aim - increasing your focus.

There are only 24 hours in every day and some of those need to be spent resting, sleeping, eating, socialising, and consumed by general hygiene tasks. However, the rest of the time you're free to focus on the things you want to do and the things you need to do. It can be very easy to focus on the things you want to do over the things you really need to do because these are more enjoyable and therefore higher up on your priority list.

However, that's a case of having the wrong priorities!

Learning how to manage your time can be complicated with all manner of time management strategies and hacks, but you can break it down to its most simplistic methods too - prioritising and scheduling.

In this chapter, we're going to simplify time management and help you see how being able to prioritise the most urgent and important task can help you feel more in control, banish stress, and therefore allow you to focus more effectively. We're also going to introduce you to the idea of scheduling, which throws the old-fashioned to-do list out of the window and creates a much more reliable way forward.

By doing this, you'll find that you get far more out of the hours you have during the day, and you'll be able to focus far more effectively as a result. When you are not in control of your daily tasks, it can be very difficult to pay the right amount of attention to anything. You're always thinking with half of your brain on what you need to do, with the other half desperately trying to stay on track.

If this sounds like your situation, learning to make the most of your time could put you back in the driving seat of control, increase your focus, and therefore allow you to make progress in whatever you're aiming towards.

How to Approach a Task in The Best Way

A task, any task, needs to be approached in the right way in order to overcome it, complete it, and learn from it. If you simply attempt to throw yourself into a task without knowing how to do it properly, it's going to take you far longer to complete and you're probably going to become a little disillusioned because of the whole situation.

instead, why not look at a task and examine the best way to approach it first, before jumping straight in?

This particular approach works best for large tasks, e.g. something you need to do which is going to take, and probably something which you don't enjoy too much. This is prime procrastination territory if you don't tread carefully, but actually working out the best way forward can help you to avoid procrastination and find a far more productive way forwards.

Look at the task and ask yourself whether it can be done in five minutes or less. If so, you need to do it there and then, getting rid of the task and therefore easing your mind.

If the task is going to take more than five minutes, ask yourself how important it is. Be honest here and don't try and give yourself extra time simply because you don't really like the task you need to do! From there, you can assess whether you need to break the task down into smaller chunks, or whether it can be done in one go.

If it can be done in one go and it's going to take you less than two hours, go for it and get it done. You'll feel a real sense of achievement and you'll have one less thing to worry about. However, anything over the two-hour mark will probably need to be broken down into smaller chunks, to enable you to focus and complete the task to the best of your ability.

So, how do you do that?

Look at the task and where it breaks up naturally. If it's a long, ongoing task, such as writing a report, estimate the time it's going to take to complete it and then divide it by a certain number of days, depending upon the deadline and how urgent it is.

It's vital that you don't fall into the trap of being unrealistic here. You cannot sit for 5 or 6 hours straight, tapping away at the keyboard trying to complete a report. You're going to end up tired, your brain is going to be screaming at you, and you'll probably end up making mistakes because of both of the above points. However, if you break it up into chunks of around 2 hours or so, you'll make slow and steady progress, and you'll find it easier to commit to the time and focus as a whole.

Learning the best way to approach a task will save you a huge amount of time, but it will also ensure that you're not wasting your own efforts by throwing time and energy at a task that simply cannot be done quickly. Some things take longer and you need to just be fine with that. Make peace with the fact that some tasks are going to take you a few days or possibly even longer, but as long as you keep tapping away at them, they will eventually be completed. You'll probably feel great when they're finished too!

There is another good option to think about here and it is called the Pomodoro Technique.

The Pomodoro Technique is a time management method that is ideal for keeping your focus on track. The reason is that you're not concentrating for endless hours, slugging away at a task that is not inspiring you in the slightest. Instead, you're challenging yourself to focus and promising yourself a break at the end of a certain amount of time.

The Pomodoro Technique was invented in the 1980s by a guy called Francesco Cirillo, and he can be thanked for many people becoming far more productive as a result of his method!

The Pomodoro Technique looks a little like this:

1. You work for a period of 25 minutes, focusing and concentrating on one task solidly and to the best of your ability. You should set your timer to 25 minutes to ensure that you don't go over this time and so you're not constantly looking at your watch and wasting time without realising it.
2. Once the alarm goes off, take a break for 5 minutes and do nothing at all. Chill out, get a drink of water, go for a walk, but do not work. The idea is that you're giving your brain a rest and allowing yourself to be refreshed enough to focus once more after the break is finished. Again, set your alarm, just in case.
3. After your break, set the alarm for another 25 minutes and work towards your next 5-minute-long break.
4. After 4 sessions like this, called Pomodoro's, you should take a longer break of between 15 to 30 minutes and try to get away from your desk completely. After that time, you start back at step one and repeat once more.

This method hinges on the fact that taking breaks is necessary for focus. You might think it's totally counterproductive to suggest that you should take a break in order to focus, but without that time to recharge and chill out, even if it is just for five minutes, you're allowing your brain to become so clogged up with thoughts and stress that you just can't think straight.

Try it once or twice and see how much extra work you get done. The fact that you have a short endpoint for your working session, after 25 minutes, makes it far more achievable and gives you something to aim towards. You could even try challenging yourself to try and see how much you can fit into those 25 minutes, although it's important that you're not unrealistic. Don't try and do too much otherwise you're going to rush and make mistakes - that's not productive at all.

How to Prioritise Effectively

Another very effective way to focus and get more done in the time you have is to prioritise.

Everyone knows how to prioritise, but not many people know how to do it effectively. For this, you can either use a list that you write down yourself, or you can use an app that you can download onto a phone or tablet. It really depends on which option you prefer as to which will work best for you. For some people, however, the extra features of an app help to motivate them to get more done, whilst other people prefer the solid action of writing something down and then actually ticking it off the list manually.

Again, it's up to you and your preferences.

So, what is prioritising?

Prioritising basically means that you're making a list of tasks that you need to complete and you're working out which order to complete them in. This is decided upon by how important or urgent they are, and not based on which tasks you like to do best. For that reason, prioritising doesn't give you space to procrastinate, because it's firmly based on importance.

Let's look at an example. We'll base this on a work situation, but you can use this same model of prioritising for absolutely anything in life, including homework, housework, or general tasks you need to complete.

Let's say that you have the following list of tasks to do, with their specific deadlines:

- Write a 10,000 word report which needs to be done by this Friday (today is Tuesday)

- Telephone a customer who complained yesterday
- Complete your tax return - the deadline is tomorrow
- Book your train journey for a conference next Monday
- Open your incoming mail
- File away a stack of papers that have been sitting in your filing tray
- Email around your team and ask for volunteers to help with a presentation to be held on Friday

Now, let's look at the order you would prioritise these tasks in and why.

- Priority 1 - Complete your tax return (Figures already inputted, just submitting and payment)
- Priority 2 - Telephone a customer who complained yesterday
- Priority 3 - Email around your team for help with Friday's presentation
- Priority 4 - Complete 2500 words of the report to be submitted on Friday
- Priority 5 - Book your train journey for Monday
- Priority 6 - Open your incoming mail
- Priority 7 - Do the filing

Let's look at why this is the best order to complete these tasks.

The tax return is without a doubt the most pressing matter on that list and therefore it needs to be prioritised as number one, completed first. If you don't complete your tax return on time you're going to end up in trouble and the deadline is tomorrow. Fix that problem and you will be free to do the rest of what is on your list.

Secondly, you need to focus on the complaint a customer filed yesterday. Leaving a complaint for too long can cause a customer to become even more irate and possibly end up taking action against your company (if applicable) and certainly leaving your business and moving to a competitor. Call the customer as your second task of the day and identify what actions need to be completed as a result of that call.

The next task is to email your team to ask for help with Friday's presentation. Whilst the presentation isn't until four days later, you're going to need to give your team time to respond to your request, so it is quite an urgent task on your list. However, it will only take around 5 minutes to do, so you can complete that without many quibbles as your third priority.

Your fourth priority of the day is the report which is due on Friday. You have four days to complete the report, so dividing the word count of 10,000 words into four (the number of days you have) will allow you to make progress, whilst also ensuring that you continue to complete the other tasks on your list. It also reduces stress and allows you to focus on the report far more effectively.

By the time you reach the fifth task on your list, it's probably coming towards mid-afternoon time and that means you can breathe a little easier knowing that your most important tasks are finished. You will feel a surge of energy and relief in knowing this and as a result, you won't struggle with mid-afternoon focus problems. Next up, you need to book your train travel for Monday. Whilst there are still a few days until your journey, we all know that prices can surge towards the date of travel, so doing it now will save you money, time and stress towards the end of the week.

Your final two tasks are relatively quick ones. First, open your incoming mail and decide what you need to do with each item. Once that is finished, you're free to spend the last hour or so of the day doing your filing, decluttering your desk for the next day.

From this example, you can see how prioritising actually works. Your most important tasks are done earlier in the day, so you're not stressing throughout the entire day and worrying that you're going to run out of time. When this happens, either the task gets put off until the next day and therefore becomes more urgent, or you end up working late and becoming tired, agitated and stressed. Neither option is a good one.

As we mentioned before, prioritising your tasks in this way can be done in any situation, and it doesn't necessarily have to be a work situation.

Write your tasks down and number them from 1 to whatever, with 1 being the most important. Then, as you complete a task, tick it off. You'll be surprised how good it feels to tick something off that list!

However, there is one thing to be wary of here - do not put too much onto your list. If you do this, you're setting yourself up for failure and you're going to feel terrible once the day has finished and your list is left incomplete. It's far better to stick to a moderate, doable amount of tasks and work your way through them, than trying to move mountains in a day.

Always be realistic if you want to be productive, but if you want to ensure that your focus remains unwavering.

When Your Day Doesn't Go According to Plan

There is something we need to address which works hand in hand with the prioritising example we've just talked about - what happens when your day doesn't go according to plan.

We've all been there. You wake up with good intentions, you're feeling positive and upbeat, and you write your list of tasks to do for the day. You're feeling like you're actually going to make progress today and your focus is razor-sharp as you start to tick items off. It feels great!

Then, out of nowhere, an urgent task comes your way and it simply cannot wait. There is no way you can put this task off until tomorrow and there is also no way you can finish this new task and all the other ones you had pencilled in too.

It's a stressful situation and one which can cause you to want to run away and forget about the day. However, you can manage it, you simply need to stay calm and be realistic.

Forget about trying to move the mountains we just warned you against here; you're not going to be able to focus when you know you have a million tasks to do within one day. Instead, take another look at your priority list and work out if any of those tasks can be moved over until tomorrow.

For instance, looking back at the list we had in our last section. You could probably move booking your train travel over until tomorrow, provided you made it a high priority the next day and you could certainly move the filing over. That may free you up enough time to work on the new task.

However, if you still don't have enough time despite moving a few things over tomorrow, with the aim not to overcrowd the next day, you might be able to delegate too.

If you're in a position to delegate tasks, this is something you can do whenever you feel overloaded, however, you should be careful not to simply pass work over to someone else on a regular basis, as they're probably going to start resenting you for it!

For that reason, only delegate when you really need to, and make sure that you delegate as little as possible.

It goes without saying that when something threatens to derail your entire day you should stay calm and positive. These things happen to the best of us, even the most productive people in the world have days when their to-do list just gets torn up and they have to get on with whatever has come their way.

So, to summarise, your main options here are:

- Reorganise your to-do list and move unimportant tasks over until tomorrow (placing them as a slightly higher priority the next day)
- Stay calm
- Delegate if possible

- Understand that this happens to everyone at some point

It can be difficult to deal with situations such as this, but remembering that life is always going throw you curveballs is important. By understanding this, you won't allow your focus to be affected and you'll be able to continue doing what you need to do, albeit slightly later than you anticipated.

What is Scheduling?

The next item to talk about is something called scheduling. This means that you're not going to procrastinate (more on that in our next chapter) and you'll feel more confident in your ability to get what you need to do, done.

Let's look at the alternative for a second, to explain scheduling in the best way.

Throughout the course of a day, when a new task comes your way, what do you do with it?

You either place it in your in-tray, you scribble it down on a piece of paper, you add it to a list on your phone of 'things to do', or you put it somewhere and probably forget about it until it becomes so urgent that you're reminded of it in no uncertain terms.

All of those methods are flawed.

By putting it in your in-tray, it's probably going to get buried under a million other tasks. If you scribble it down, you might lose that piece of paper and by adding it to a list on your phone, it's going to get lost in the melee. If you put it somewhere, you might lose it.

Instead, why not schedule in a time to complete it and then commit to actually doing it?

Let's give an example to demonstrate scheduling clearly.

You receive your annual letter from the Tax Office that your tax return is due on 31 January at the latest. If you're self-employed, you'll be very familiar with this letter or notification.

It's vital that you don't forget this because if you do, you're going to be in big trouble.

You might be tempted to think "oh that's months away, I'll remember", but what if you don't remember? What if you wake up on 1 February and suddenly panic because you just remembered the letter you received a few months ago?

You might also simply put it on your phone's to-do list app, assuming that you'll remember to do it in good time. Again, this is a possibly flawed idea.

Instead, scheduling will ensure that you have the time to complete the task and that you don't forget it.

It goes a little like this.

1. You receive the letter from the Tax Office and you see the date that your return needs to be submitted by
2. You look any your calendar, either a diary or an app, and one month before you block out a period of time to complete your return. Now, you know how long your particular tax return is going to take so make sure that you're realistic with the amount of time you block out; it could be that you need to block out more than one session over a day or so
3. Set an alert on your app to remind you to complete the task or get yourself into a routine of looking at your diary every day for any particular tasks you've scheduled in
4. When the time arrives - do it! No excuses, just do what you've scheduled in

That's it! Scheduling means that rather than writing a task down to be done at some point in the future, you actually make time for it and therefore get it done.

There are a few points of caution to remember here. For instance, if the task you are scheduling in is going to require you travelling somewhere to actually do it, such as a meeting or going to see a friend for coffee, then you need to schedule in an amount of time which reflects this too. Don't just block in an hour for the meeting and totally forget about half an hour travel there and half an hour back!

You should also always be realistic with whatever you time block into your schedule. You are not superhuman! Remember that you have a life outside of work or whatever responsibilities you have, so you need to eat, sleep, shower, relax, and have a social life too! You might be tempted to schedule in absolutely everything because it gives you peace of mind that you haven't forgotten anything, but you still need space in your diary to be a little spontaneous from time to time - that's part of what makes life fun!

By using scheduling in this way, you're taking the stress out of trying to remember things, which unburdens your mind. How does this fit into focus? It allows you to be free to pay attention to whatever task you have in front of you.

It's impossible to focus when your mind is blocked, something we've discussed at length already. By using these time management methods, and by ensuring that you make time for yourself within it, you're allowing your focus levels to naturally increase and therefore ensuring you remain productive.

Points to Remember From This Chapter

This chapter has been a bumper one, but it's packed with very useful and usable advice you can take forwards and work into your day.

Most of us struggle with not having enough hours in the day from time to time, and when you have a list of tasks to complete and not enough time to do them, it's easy to become stressed and find it hard to focus and concentrate on whatever is in front of you. By being more organised with your time and trying to work out the best way to approach a task, you're making solid progress and ensuring your focus remains sharp.

The main points to take from this chapter are:

- Focus can be seriously affected by the way you manage your time

- Understand that you can only do so much within a day and you are not superhuman - just focus on doing the best you can do
- Look at each task and work out the best way to approach it, in order to help you save time and actually complete what you need to do more effectively
- Time management techniques, such as the Pomodoro Technique, are very useful for keeping you on track and also enforcing the idea that breaks are not counterproductive and can actually help you focus more effectively
- Prioritising the tasks you need to do in order of urgency and importance will help you do more in the time you have and allows your focus to remain sharp
- Always be realistic with what you can do; trying to do too much will simply zap your energy and cause you to procrastinate
- Understand and accept that sometimes your day will go wrong and things will come to send your plans awry, but this isn't a reason to give up and worry about it. Simply re-adjust and try again.

Chapter 6:
Your Number One Enemy - Procrastination

If there is one thing to throw all your plans off course, it's procrastination.

Procrastination goes around loving the idea of making your plans go awry; it loves the idea that you're putting things off and then worrying about them at a later date, and it adores the stress it causes when that later date arrives, and you have no time left.

Procrastination is the energy of your time, your focus, and your productiveness.

We've mentioned procrastination in passing a few times throughout the book and especially in our last chapter on prioritising and scheduling, but we need to do a real deep dive on this subject, such is its importance.

You will not be able to focus if you allow procrastination into your life. It's also entirely possible that the reason you are struggling with maintaining focus is all down to your procrastination habits.

Now, don't worry if you're prone to doing this; you shouldn't feel guilty about it and you shouldn't worry about it too much, simply because you're about to do something about it. If you choose to continue down a road towards constant procrastination however, that's when you need to worry!

This chapter is going to explore the deeper meaning of procrastination, understanding why it's not a good thing to have in your life, whilst also talking about the other enemy you need to be aware of - perfectionism. If you're someone who is always trying to be perfect, or you're always comparing yourself to others and coming up short, it's time to throw that habit out of the window and accept yourself as the wonderful being you are. How does this help with focus? That's something we're going to explore in this chapter!

For now, let's do some defining.

What is Procrastination?

Procrastination is basically the art of putting something off until tomorrow. There are many reasons for doing this, but the main ones are that a task is either unpleasant, you're not sure how to do it, or that you feel it's too large and you're not sure where to begin.

None of those are the greatest reasons for not doing something, but procrastination is something we all do from time to time, some more often than others. It's an easy option, and as a result, we find it easier to fall foul of it because it's less trouble than actually doing the thing we're trying to avoid. It sounds confusing, but without a doubt, it's something you do on an at least regular basis.

So, do you procrastinate regularly? Be honest, there's no judgement here, and the only way to change a negative habit is to face up to it and acknowledge it first and foremost.

It's okay if you do procrastinate; it's not okay if after reading this chapter you continue to do it mindfully. The reason is that perhaps you're doing it and you're not aware of what you're doing. Part and parcel of procrastination is that you're telling yourself it's okay not to do something by legitimising it with another reason.

For instance, you might put off writing a report until tomorrow, probably because it's a large job and you don't really like writing reports. You tell yourself that if you focus the entire day on it tomorrow, you'll get more done and you're more likely to complete it on time. The payoff, you tell yourself, is that you'll complete all your smaller jobs today, giving you a constant hit of happiness because you're ticking items off your to-do list left, right, and centre.

Yes, you're actually getting something done, so in many ways, you're being productive, but you're not placing your attention where it needs to be. As a result, the most urgent job, i.e. the report, isn't being done and when the deadline comes around, you're going to be rushing, stressed out, likely to miss the deadline and also likely to make mistakes.

Procrastination can be damaging on many levels and it can cause a huge amount of stress to build up. The longer you procrastinate, the worst it becomes, and the more unproductive and unable to focus you are. When this is allowed to fester, you end up with a workload that is totally unmanageable and the stress rises to unbearable levels. Over time, this can become extremely damaging to your physical and mental health.

We've mentioned a few times that when you're feeling stressed about something, it's hard to pay close attention to it, i.e. you can't focus as well as you should be able to, or as much as you want to. This is frustrating, causes a vicious circle of feeling bad about yourself, and therefore leads to more stress and, in the end, more procrastination.

Over the long-term procrastination can become a very negative habit, because you tell yourself that by not doing a task, you're going to do something better. You're almost legitimising it, but in the falsest of ways. You're lying to yourself because all you're actually doing is making your future harder, even if that future is only tomorrow.

This chapter is going to address the big P and help you learn techniques to actually kick it out of your life as much as possible. We'll say 'as much as possible' because we're all human. At some point you're probably going to procrastinate again but provided it's only on a very small task that isn't going to cause any major drama, you shouldn't have to worry. It's when you allow the habit of procrastination to start creeping back into your life that you need to take solid action to reduce its effects and get rid of it once more.

So, before we move on, ask yourself honestly whether you procrastinate on a regular basis and try and work out the types of things you regularly procrastinate on. By doing that, you'll be able to dedicate the advice we're going to give to your particular situation in a clearer way.

Is it work? Studying? Housework? Bill paying? Identify if you have a particular troubleshooting area or whether you have a tendency to generally procrastinate. The more honest you are with yourself, the more you have to work with. This allows you to make changes that will benefit you now and in the future.

5 Ways to Avoid Procrastination

Even though procrastination is extremely easy to do, and it's something we all fall foul of occasionally, there are a few ways to help reduce its effects and even work to kick it out of your life in general. The more you practice less procrastination, the easier it becomes.

You've taken the first step by being mindful of the fact that you actually procrastinate. That's something to pat yourself on the back for; identifying the source problem at hand is half of the battle.

In this section, we're going to talk at length about five specific techniques you can use to avoid falling into a procrastination trap. It could be that all five techniques work for you, or it could be that just one or two are effective. Remember, we're all different and there is no one size fits all answer to this boosting focus business! You can, however, give all five techniques a try and see which one suits you best - one is sure to!

Question Your Motivation

The first technique we're going to cover is questioning your motivation and asking yourself why you want to put the task off, i.e. why you want to procrastinate. This particular method hinges on you actually recognising that you're about to procrastinate, so you need to be quite mindful in order for this to work.

So, how do you do that? How do you actually recognise that procrastination is at hand?

You have to know yourself, put simply. As you are making decisions over what to do and what to do later, ask yourself "am I procrastinating?" You will know if you are because you're putting off a task that should be done right now, or can be done right now, until a later date. From there, you need to find out the reason why.

Questioning your motivation means analysing the reason for procrastinating. Is it because you don't like the task you need to do? Is it because you haven't done this task before and you're not sure how to do it? Is it because it's a big task and looking at it seems like your personal Everest? Is it because you're feeling tired and you just don't want to do anything?

Question your reason for putting this task off and falling foul of procrastination. Once you know why you're doing something, you can tackle reasons at source and work out a way around it.

Let's look at each potential motivation/reason in turn and work out how to deal with it.

- **You don't like the task** - Probably reason number one for procrastinating! When you don't like doing something, it's very hard to focus on it. However, we all have to do things we don't like occasionally, so try focusing on the end result instead. Imagine how good it's going to feel when the task is complete and hold onto that idea to get you through to the end. You could also try delayed gratification if all else fails; that means promising yourself a reward at the end of the task. That might be enough to motivate you to avoid procrastinating and just get it done.
- **You don't know how to do the task** - You cannot be expected to know how to do everything, so if the reason for procrastinating is that you don't know how to do it, change your mindset and look towards a learning opportunity instead. Ask a colleague to show you what to do, or do a

little research into it. Who knows, you might actually enjoy the task once you've learnt how to do it! Tell yourself that this is a chance to expand your skills and knowledge.

- **It seems like the task is too big and you don't know where to start** - Another hugely common reason for procrastinating. Big tasks can seem like mountains and you're looking up at the summit, thinking it's impossible to get there. It's not impossible, you simply need to approach it in a different way. Break the task down into manageable chunks and work on a section at a time. With each completed section, celebrate a little and pat yourself on the back. This may be enough to motivate you towards the end of the task, and because it no longer seems like a huge mountain to climb, you'll find it easier to focus too.
- **You just don't feel like doing anything** - If this is the case, you need to ask yourself why. Are you not getting enough sleep? Are you feeling ill? Sometimes we need to just focus on self-care and invest in tomorrow. If you're feeling sluggish and lacking in energy, just do what you can and don't beat yourself up for the things you can't do. However, if you're simply feeling lazy and there's no real reason for it, you need to motivate yourself to get moving! In this case, the techniques we're doing to talk about from this point on should be useful to you.

By understanding your motivation for procrastinating, you can work towards giving yourself a boost of energy, boosting your focus as a result, and therefore avoiding falling foul of this rather unproductive and quite stressful habit.

Time Challenges

Time challenges are a great strategy if you're feeling sluggish, tired, or you just don't like doing a specific task. In this case, you challenge yourself to complete a specific task within a certain amount of time. There are a few guidelines to this strategy, however.

Firstly, you need to be familiar with the task so you can estimate a realistic amount of time you're going to need to complete it. You cannot take a task that realistically takes an hour to complete to a high standard and expect to be able to do it 20 minutes. That's not going to work, you're going to struggle, and then you're going to feel like you've failed, which means procrastination has won.

Instead, take a task and work out how long it is going to take you, being realistic in your estimation. Then, perhaps shave 5 minutes of the time. Then, set your clock and work flat out to hit your target.

This particular technique works well because it hits your competitive streak. Everyone has one; sure, it might be that yours is a little well buried, or your friends are a little more competitive than you, but challenging yourself to do something and feel good about achieving it is something work motivating yourself for.

During the time you're challenging yourself, make sure you give it maximum focus. Turn off your phone, don't allow distractions to enter the room and really work to hit your target.

When you hit it, which you probably will, congratulate yourself and reward yourself in some way. It might be a simple pat on the back, it might be a half an hour break, it could be your favourite chocolate bar, or it could be going outside for a walk in the fresh air. This reward will also help to motivate you, but make sure that you're sticking with healthy rewards and you're not going over the top. You're trying to kick an unhealthy procrastination habit, not replace it with another one!

Eat That Frog

Before you panic, you're not actually expected to eat a frog, or anything for that matter. The title of this particular strategy is merely symbolic!

If you were to eat a frog, we would imagine it would be quite unpleasant. So, if you really had to do it, you'd want to get it out of the way pretty early in the day, to ensure it wasn't sitting on your mind all day, causing you to worry and feel stressed out. The idea of actually having to eat a slimy frog would no doubt cause you to put other tasks off, therefore procrastinating, and you wouldn't be able to focus on anything else in the process.

But, if you ate the frog and got it over and done with early in the day, you would feel relieved that it was over and you could then focus on the tasks you had to do for the rest of the day.

Right?

Well, that's basically what Eat the Frog means, without any consumption of slimy living creatures.

The frog is the task that you really don't like or don't want to do, and you would get it over and done with by completing it early in the day, to avoid it becoming a huge focus-blocker for the rest of your time.

Identifying your personal frog isn't difficult. Think about the tasks you need to do that day and the one that makes you feel 'yuck', or 'urgh' is your frog. It's the task you don't enjoy, the one that's boring, or the one that you generally dislike. Do it, forget about it, and then move on with your day.

The idea behind this particular strategy is that the 'frog' in your day causes you a mental block and as a result, you simply can't focus on anything else. Your mind is stuck on the thing you have to do later that you really don't like or don't want to do. This focus-block causes you to be massively unproductive, slow, and unable to think about anything else. It might not be that dramatic in effect, but the block will be enough to slow you down at least.

Imagine Tomorrow

A good way to avoid procrastination is to imagine what tomorrow is going to be like if you don't do what you're supposed to do today. You might try and tell yourself that you'll get up earlier and you'll work a bit longer to compensate, but be realistic here. Will you really? No. And, as a result, you'll end up feeling ten times more tired and stressed out because you didn't halve your workload today.

The problem with procrastination is that it whispers in your ear and makes you think that putting something off isn't a terrible idea, it's totally do-able and something you should be able to decide for yourself. Sure, it is something you can decide, but it is going to make tomorrow worse? Probably so.

Sit down and realistically try and visualise how you're going to feel tomorrow when you're faced with all the work you have to do; plus the task you didn't do today. For a second, try and imagine how stressed you're going to feel and how pressed for time you will be.

Don't allow those thoughts of "ah, it'll be fine" to creep in, because we all know it won't be! The likelihood is that you'll end up putting off a task you were supposed to do tomorrow until the next day, causing a snowball effect that will last for days. It's also possible that you won't even do the task you're procrastinating on, and it will be delayed for even more days, which makes the whole thing ten times more stressful in the end.

Visualising the next day and experiencing those mock-negative feelings may be enough to force you to just get the task over and done with today. When you've done it, you'll be glad you did and you'll feel proud and accomplished as a result.

Set Realistic Goals

In our last chapter, we talked about writing down all the tasks you need to complete and prioritising them in order to complete them correctly. This is a little different but works along the same lines.

Every day, look at your task list and set goals that are realistic. For instance, tell yourself that you will type up half of the 7000 word report today and half tomorrow. That is a realistic goal that you can complete and then tomorrow, you'll be able to completely tick that task off your to-do list.

Another thing you should bear in mind is that you factor in breaks. Do you remember in the last chapter we talked about the Pomodoro Technique? That particular technique is successful because it uses timed sessions of total focus with small breaks included. Breaks are not optional, they are small amounts of time your brain needs to refresh and refocus. Without breaks, the focus will go completely out of the window.

So, when you're setting your goals, make sure that you factor in some break time too, to allow yourself to breathing space you need to feel clearer and more productive overall.

Learning That Perfectionism Isn't Real

Before we wrap this chapter up, we need to focus on another P word - perfectionism.

You might wonder how trying to hit perfection targets every day could cause you to have less focus, but it's actually one of the biggest culprits.

When you try and be perfect all the time, you fail. The reason is that you cannot be perfect all the time, and what is perfection anyway? Is it looking a certain way? Is it completing every task you have? Is it hitting a certain standard?

Perfection doesn't exist, so in trying to reach it, you're actually scrambling around the dark, trying to find a target that has no definition.

How many times per day do you compare yourself to other people? We all do it and social media certainly hasn't made it any easier to avoid. However, by comparing yourself to other people you're selling yourself short every single time. Why are they better than you? The truth is that they're not, but you see them as being that way, so you instantly feel bad about yourself.

When you feel bad, you can't focus. It's that simple.

Negativity is a thief of happiness, contentment, motivation, productivity, and focus too.

Instead of trying to hit so-called perfectionism, why not simply focus on doing your best? As long as you're trying your hardest and you're doing your best every single day, that's really all you can expect or ask for. In many ways, that's what real perfectionism is - the very best you can do in the time you have, in the way you're feeling in that particular moment, and with the tools you have to hand.

In many ways, trying to reach perfection standards actually causes you to procrastinate. The reason is that you're trying to reach something that's impossible, so you see no real point in attempting it. As a result, you put tasks off and tell yourself you'll do them tomorrow, or the next day, but the reality is you could have just done them as well as you could and it would have been more than enough. It would have been your version of perfection and no procrastination would have come into it.

Forget trying to be perfect. Instead, focus on just doing your best.

Points to Remember From This Chapter

This chapter has been a huge lesson on procrastination, before ending with a little pep talk on avoiding perfectionism. Hopefully, by this point, you'll be feeling motivated and upbeat, and understanding that increasing your focus really comes down to changing many different elements of how you do things, how you think, and the habits you develop. There's no single method for increasing your focus; it comes down to several different sub-sections of action you need to take.

The main points from this chapter are:

- Procrastination means that you put a task off until tomorrow, or a later date, because you either don't want to do it, don't know how to do it, or it seems like too big a task to tackle
- Procrastination can severely damage your productivity and your focus
- The more you procrastinate, the more stressed out you will feel
- Recognising that you are actually procrastinating is a huge part of the story
- Understand that perfection doesn't exist and that by attempting to reach it you're basically setting yourself up for failure
- It's far better to focus on simply doing your best than trying to be perfect
- You can try and kick procrastination out of your life by being more time organised, taking regular breaks, performing less desirable tasks early in the day, and by challenging yourself to get a specific task done in a specific amount of time.

Chapter 7:
Is Your Lifestyle Affecting Your Focus?

In our next chapter, our final chapter, we're going to talk at length about specific strategies you can use to keep your focus levels high, and therefore allow you to do more in the time you have, in a higher quality way. However, there is one thing we need to talk about before we get there - your lifestyle.

Did you know that your habits and the way you live your life can have a huge effect on your ability to focus and concentrate? A good lifestyle gives you the tools you need to keep your brain sharp and active, however, a poor lifestyle does the total opposite and makes it feel like you're swimming in mud every single day, unable to really get much done of substance. This is a fast track towards stress in many ways, and we've already addressed the fact that stress does nothing for your focus!

So, what areas do you need to address in terms of having the best type of lifestyle for added focus and concentration?

- Eating a healthy, varied diet
- Exercising on a regular basis
- Ensuring a regular, quality sleeping pattern

This chapter is going to talk about the above three points at length and help you make any specific changes you need. By doing that, and working with the strategies we're going to cover in our next chapter, you'll find that your efforts are definitely not in vain.

Let's start with what you fuel your brain and body with on a daily basis.

Top Foods For Focus

Have you ever heard of the saying "you are what you eat?" In terms of brain function, there couldn't be a truer word said!

If you feed your brain with the vitamins and minerals it needs to stay sharp and active, it will reward you with total focus. This enables you to reach your goals, tick off your deadlines, and be completely energised physically and mentally.

So, what foods should you be adding to your diet if you want to maintain and improve your mental focus and sharpness?

- **Berries, particularly blueberries** - Blueberries, in particular, are not only delicious but they also contain powerful antioxidants that can help to stimulate the flow of oxygen and blood to the brain. In addition, the range of antioxidants contained with blueberries can also stimulate the brain and give you added focus, simply by eating a rather delicious serving on top of your morning porridge!

- **Green tea** - You've no doubt heard a lot about green tea over the last few years and it's the ability to help you lose weight, but it has other benefits too. One of those is the ability to increase your focus. Green tea contains caffeine and we all know that it is ideal for waking you up in the morning and giving you a kick of mental energy. However, it also contains something called L-Theanine which regulates the caffeine delivery, therefore meaning that you're not going to have an energy high, followed by a crash.

- **Leafy greens** - Make sure you get a good serving of leafy green vegetables every day as these have a huge number of health benefits. They also contain a range of different antioxidants and also carotenoids, which combine together to give your brain a boost, allowing you to focus more intensely, for longer. In addition, leafy greens are a good source of natural folic acid, which is another brain booster.

- **Avocados** - Having enjoyed a serious popularity boost over the last few years, avocados aren't just rather delicious and give your food a pretty green hue, they're also fantastic for boosting blood flow to the brain, which delivers important nutrients and oxygen. This basically means increased brainpower and the ability to focus for much longer.
- **Fatty or oily fish** - This type of fish (namely mackerel, herring, salmon and trout) contains omega 3 fatty acids which are a must-have for top brain function. Regular consumption (a few times a week) could boost your brainpower and help you to focus for longer.
- **Dark chocolate (in moderation)** - Before you go grabbing a huge bar of dark chocolate and assuming you can eat it all, this basically means a square or two a day and nothing more! When eaten in moderation, dark chocolate could boost your brainpower because of the antioxidants contained within it. There is a little caffeine in dark chocolate, which we know is good for focus, but magnesium is also included which relaxes you and makes you feel less stressed; this is also ideal for focus.
- **Water** - We all know that staying hydrated is important, but it has a lot of benefits for brain health and power too. You can think deeper, for longer, and focus better when you're well-hydrated, so make sure that you get enough water

every day. The general recommendation is 8 x 8oz glasses per day.

- **Nuts** - Aside from being a far healthier snack than sugary sweets, nuts are a good source of vitamin E which helps to protect your brain as you age. The vitamins and minerals contained in nuts can also help you to focus because of the natural amino acids and essential oils contained within them. However, be sure to avoid the salty varieties, as these aren't at all healthy!
- **Flax seeds** - Finally, we have lax seeds which are fantastically high in different vitamins and minerals, such as magnesium, the aforementioned omega 3 fatty acids, fibre and several types of vitamin B. All of these help your brainpower, but they're also very healthy in general too.

The good news is that none of these foods and beverages are particularly hard to find or difficult to eat. You can easily sprinkle some flax seeds on your breakfast or on your salad at lunch, or you can snack on them throughout the day. You can snack on nuts, you can have a square of dark chocolate as a treat after dinner, and the rest can easily be incorporated into your day too.

It really comes down to having a varied and healthy diet and ensuring that you incorporate these known focus-boosters into your day.

Why Exercise is Important

It's not just about what you eat, but how often you move too! This is true for general health, but exercise also has a very important effect on the brain, and therefore on your ability to focus.

Have you ever noticed that after you've had some exercise, perhaps a walk around the block at lunchtime, that you return to your desk feeling energised and you're able to focus far better? This isn't an accident, it's completely predictable; when you exercise, you increase blood flow to your brain, ensuring that oxygen and other nutrients are able to get where they need to be. In addition, you're de-stressing, because exercise is a known stress management technique.

You don't have to head to the gym to get the benefits you need; you can simply go for a quick ten minutes' walk! However, if you want to make your exercise efforts a bit more focused and structured, then how about an exercise class with friends once or twice a week? You could join a team sport, or you could join the gym and go with a friend or family member for a boost of social action.

The more exercise you get, the healthier you'll be, not only physically, but mentally too. Many studies have shown that when you exercise, you're able to remember more too, which is also useful when you're trying to focus on a task and do it to the best of your ability. This all comes down to the endorphins, which are released during exercise, which give you a boost of brain health and function.

Once you've finished exercising, studies have also shown that you can focus more easily, you're less distracted, and you can pay more attention to what you're trying to do. Your memory improves when your body is active, and this is the perfect storm for overall increased brain focus and function.

If you're trying to improve your work focus, why not head out for a walk at lunchtime instead of sitting in the break room and scrolling through social media? Alternatively, first thing in the morning is a great time to get your day's exercise in, as it will start the day in the best possible way and allow you to retain your focus throughout the morning, which is often the toughest part of the day for many people.

You could go for a morning swim, you could walk to work rather than taking the car or the bus, or you could hit the gym if you're feeling really active!

Of course, you need to enjoy the exercise you're doing, so choose something which stands out to you and something which you enjoy. If you hate running, it's simple - don't run! If you love to swim, then go ahead and be a human dolphin, swimming as much as you want! Provided you enjoy the activity, it gets your heart rate up and makes you only slightly out of the breath when you're doing it, it's working and it's giving you benefits.

You don't have to pound the treadmill to get the beneficial effects of exercise!

Sleep, Glorious Sleep!

The next lifestyle point to make is regarding sleep.

How many of you regularly get between 7 to 8 hours of uninterrupted sleep every single night, without fail?

There probably aren't so many hands in the air right now.

Modern society forces us to be constantly switched on, whether that's on social media or via a smartphone connected to another type of messaging app. We're never still!

This can have a huge effect on your sleep levels, and the fact is that if you want to be able to focus and achieve more in the time you have, you need to be well-rested. This means getting between 7 to 8 hours of good quality sleep every single night, assuming you're an adult.

If you regularly find it hard to get to sleep, you're waking up several times during the night, or you have regular nights where you don't sleep at all, it's a good idea to look at your sleeping routine and make some changes. If that doesn't work, you should go and have a chat with your doctor, to find out if there is another reason why you're finding it so hard to sleep.

This is an unsurprisingly common problem of the modern-day, but that doesn't mean it's something you should put up with. Sleep deprivation is extremely damaging to health, both physically and mentally, and it only takes a night or two of poor quality sleep to cause you to go into the deprivation bracket. You then find yourself in a sleep debt, and it takes a long time to pay it back.

The following points may help you to change your sleep routine and therefore work towards a regularly good quality amount of shut-eye.

- Make sure that you go to bed at the same time every night and you set your alarm to wake up at the same time. Even if you're not working the next day, make sure you stick to this routine. It's tempting to stay in bed for an extra hour at the weekends, but this can damage your routine and cause your body clock to go haywire.

- Avoid anything too stimulating in the hours before bed, such as action and horror films, loud music, social media, etc. Instead, avoid any type of stimulation before you sleep and try reading a book or listening to relaxing music.
- Avoid eating anything heavy before bed, and if possible don't eat for 4 to 5 hours before bed. This is because digestion can greatly affect your sleep levels and if you eat a heavy meal, you're probably going to find that it affects your ability to sleep well.
- Try having a warm bath before you go to bed and see if that helps to relax you enough to fall asleep naturally.
- Look at your sleeping environment - do you have enough blankets? Do you have too many? Is the room too hot or too cold? Even the slightest detail can be enough to cause a light sleeper to have a poor night's shut-eye.
- Check your pillows; are they older than two years of age? If so, you need to replace them as they're not going to be as supportive as they were. Typically, pillows have a lifespan of between 1 to 2 years and it could be that an uncomfortable pillow is causing you to have problems sleeping.
- Try a weighted blanket if you need the feeling of extra security to fall asleep. These are typically used by people who have restless legs syndrome (RLS) but they can be used for insomnia and other sleeping problems. In this case, the blanket

is a little heavier than normal (you can purchase different weights) and they can mimic the feeling of being hugged. As a result, your body releases the feel-good hormone oxytocin, and this helps you to relax and hopefully nod off to sleep.
- Try a warm milky drink before bed, or perhaps try essential oils. Some people find a drop of lavender oil on their pillow can be enough to help them relax, although you should certainly check with your doctor before you start to use essential oils or any other sleeping aids.

This advice should help you to have a better night's sleep, but again, if you are struggling then perhaps a chat with your doctor may be called for, to ensure that you're not suffering from an underlying condition that might be helped in a different way.

When you're well-rested, you'll find it much easier to focus. However, this is something you need to repeat night after night to ensure the benefits and effects are ongoing.

A Word About Mental Health

We've talked at length about feeding your brain with different foods and beverages, and we've talked about exercise and sleep, but we haven't really mentioned too much about mental health. It's vital that we do talk about this because it's such an important subject.

We know that stress is bad, and we know that when you become overwhelmed and stressed out, it's easy for anxiety and depression to creep in. Everyone has mental health, just as everyone has physical health, but we don't talk about it as openly. That's a mistake - everyone should be free to discuss mental health in the same way as if you had broken an arm or you had bumped your head. There is still a rather worrying stigma around mental health that needs to be broken immediately.

Poor mental health can have an extremely detrimental effect on focus. We have fleetingly mentioned about depression in our time management chapter, and if you're bogged down with feelings of low confidence, low mood, worthlessness and anxiety, it's almost impossible to focus your mind on anything other than the way you're feeling. Everything seems pointless in that case.

Even if you only take a few points from this book, make this one part of that collection - if you feel that you are struggling with any element of your mental health and that is the reason for your lack of focus, go and talk to your doctor. We've mentioned it before - asking for help is a strength and not a weakness, and it will be the bravest and most worthwhile thing you ever do in your life.

Poor mental health is one of the most common reasons for a lack of focus for many people. When everything is drowning in negativity, you won't see the point in motivating yourself to do anything. The problem is, when you fall foul of that, you're creating a vicious circle that goes around and around once more.

Motivation goes out of the window and as a result, the ability to focus goes with it. You lack productivity and the frustration that you can't focus creates anger and hostility within yourself. You beat yourself up for your inability to get things done, and this gives the depression even more fuel to its fire. The only way to douse these flames is with help, support, and a huge dose of new positivity.

Dealing with mental health isn't easy, but it's something that can be done with time and effort. Part of this comes from within, part of it comes from outside and in some cases, another bout might come from treatment methods. These are things you can talk about with your doctor and find the right fit for you. However, the most important thing is that you seek help and advice if you do feel that you're struggling.

Don't tell yourself that you have to fight your way through it, don't assume you're wasting anyone's time, and don't think that you can beat it with willpower alone. Mental health conditions, when left to grow, have the power to swallow you whole. However, they can also be knocked into oblivion with the right help and support.

The ironic thing is that once you've overcome a mental health problem, you'll feel a sense of achievement in some way. Of course, for some people the battle is ongoing, but once you start to feel brighter and as though there is light at the end of the tunnel, the darkness starts to dissipate and your ability to focus and get things done starts to return.

It's almost like winter melting away for spring to arrive, and it's a wonderful feeling.

Whilst you can't automatically say that a lack of focus is down to a mental health problem, it's something to bear in mind and seek help for if you feel it might be a situation you need to address. You should, however never attempt to do this alone - there is plenty of help and support out there, you simply need to ask.

Points to Remember From This Chapter

This chapter has outlined the fact that your lifestyle dictates whether or not you're able to focus to a large degree. By looking at your lifestyle and making any necessary changes, you may find that your focus is improved quite quickly and dramatically.

Everyone can stand to make changes to their lifestyle; nobody lives perfectly! In today's age, it's very likely that you're not getting the amount of sleep you need or you're eating a poor diet, perhaps not getting enough exercise. By being honest about your lifestyle and making changes, your focus may improve.

The main points to remember from this chapter are:

- Your lifestyle has an effect on your ability to focus
- There are certain foods and beverages which are known to help boost focus and concentration and adding these to your diet isn't difficult, simply because they're not particularly obscure foods to find and enjoy
- Exercise can help boost your focus by stimulating the flow of blood, oxygen and vitamins to your brain

- Choose an exercise you enjoy and incorporate it into your routine, to notice beneficial effects on your focus levels
- If you're not getting enough sleep every night, you're going to find it hard to focus
- Sleep deprivation is a serious condition which can become an issue after just one or two poor nights of sleep
- Changing your sleeping routine may be enough to help you get a better night's sleep night after night
- If you're struggling with insomnia or poor-quality sleep, it might be a good idea to have a chat with your doctor, to ensure there are no underlying conditions which are causing you to have sleep problems
- Mental health is something you also have to pay attention to and seek help and advice for if you feel you are struggling.

Chapter 8:
Improve Your Focus Today!

We've done all the background work, now it's time to get practical!

This chapter is going to be quite the bumper one, but it's a chapter that is designed to give you the serious low-down on strategies and tactics you can use to boost your focus and get more done in the time you have.

We've already covered some practical elements, which you shouldn't forget about, such as making changes to your lifestyle, ensuring you get enough sleep on a nightly basis, using time management techniques such as the Pomodoro Technique, and trying your best to avoid procrastination.

If you use those techniques on a daily basis and then add in the strategies we're going to talk about next, you'll find that your focus is greatly improved and you're more able to pay attention to, and concentrate, on the task at hand. By doing this, you can hit those deadlines, stay in control of your work, and as a result, feel far less stressed as a result.

You might have your own reasons for wanting to boost your natural focus levels, or you might simply want to avoid feeling overwhelmed because you can't seem to pay attention for too long. We all go through times like that; you have a task that you know you need to finish, but it seems to be your own personal Everest. No matter how hard you try and get it done, you just can't seem to focus. Your brain wanders, your mind thinks of other things, and before you know it, you've convinced yourself you can't do it and you're super-ed as a result.

Increasing your focus means that situations such as that won't happen anywhere near as often if they even happen at all.

Remember, lifestyle is something you should start with first and foremost. A solid lifestyle is a foundation you can build upon, so make sure you're eating a healthy diet and you're incorporating some of the foods we talked about in our last chapter. Choose an exercise you enjoy and do it regularly and definitely make sure that you're sleeping at least 7 to 8 hours every single night.

11 Strategies to Naturally Increase Your Focus

The strategies we're about to talk about can be used on a daily basis, or you can use them when you're feeling like your focus needs a bit of a boost. They might all work wonderfully well for you, or it might be that some just don't click as much as others for you.

Just because your friend gets on well with one strategy doesn't mean you will; we're all different and unique, and that means there is no one size fits all answer to this issue. However, the range of strategies we're going to talk about throughout this bumper chapter means that you're sure to find at least a few which you can fall back on during tough times.

Our chosen 11 strategies are:

- Try a Digital Detox
- Identify and Cut Out Regular Distractions
- Learn to Invest in Yourself
- Find a New Hobby And Work to be The Best You Can
- Identify What is Important to You
- Remember That Breaks Are Important
- Try Mindfulness Meditation

- Set Small Goals on a Daily Basis
- Change Your Environment
- Avoid Multi-Tasking at All Costs
- Use Brain Training Exercises

It might be that by simply looking at that list you can identify a few you like the sound of, but read through our theory on all of them and be open-minded. Give them all a try at least once, before you choose the one or ones that you want to take forward and use whenever you feel the need.

Let's begin!

Try a Digital Detox

How often do you use your phone? Are you always on your tablet? How about your laptop? Do you use a desktop computer at work or at school? When you return home, are you bombarded by the TV?

We are all on total digital overload and we don't even realise it!

Let me ask you a question - how many hours per day do you spend on social media collectively? When you add up all the time you spend scrolling, liking, and posting, does it run into several hours? It's likely to, and the sad thing is that you're not alone in that either! Most people spend far too long on their social media platforms, to the point where there is a very real worry that social media addiction could be a new trend.

Our first suggested technique is to try a digital detox. This doesn't mean you cannot do anything which involves an item of technology, but it means being mindful of the things you regularly use and working to reduce them, by cutting them out completely and then perhaps reintroducing them in a slow and steady manner.

Why does this affect focus?

Our digital lives are a huge distraction. You might be working away on your laptop and have your phone right next to you. Every time your phone pings you want to check it. Every few minutes you might wonder whether you're missing out on something on social media. You have literal FOMO and it's not healthy!

The bottom line is that if something is that important, you will find out about it and you won't have to go in search of the news. Phones were invented as a means of communication, i.e. if something was urgent or in order to stay in touch with family and friends. They were not invented so that we could become almost attached to them, searching through social media pages and watching videos of cute cats!

Before you panic, your digital detox isn't for life, and it isn't going to include everything technological. If you need a laptop or tablet for work, then, of course, you need to use it, and the same goes for your studies. However, you need to be mindful of when your use moves from necessary to simply frivolous.

What this detox certainly does pertain to is your phone. Yes, you are going on social media blackout for a while, and it's going to hurt at first!

Try this:

- Think carefully about the amount of time you spend on social media in particular, but also include watching videos on YouTube, Netflix, etc
- Acknowledge that having your phone beside you and being in contact all the time is not a healthy action and you need to be able to switch off in order to focus and concentrate
- Log out of your social media accounts, so you are not receiving notifications (terrifying, possibly, but do it!)
- Stay logged out and do not check anything for one week
- Use that week to focus on yourself, find other hobbies and rest up

- After one week, see how you feel and assess whether you feel less ed an overwhelmed, compared to when you started out
- If you really want to, log back into your accounts and spend half an hour using them, before logging out again. You are able to give yourself half an hour per day on social media, so you need to identify a suitable half an hour throughout the day and plan it into your routine
- If you find that you didn't miss social media and you're not really that bothered about using it again, that's even better!

Now, if you use social media accounts for your work then you need to log out of your personal accounts and only use your business accounts. However, if these are interchangeable or you don't have a business page set up, that's something you need to do before you can attempt your digital detox.

Once you've done that, turn off notifications and limit checking messages and other notifications to twice per day and for no longer than half an hour in total.

You will be able to focus far better if you don't have your phone at the side of you, with messages and notifications pinging left, right and centre, but there is another point to consider here too - social media and other technological endeavours can be mental baggage and blocks.

It's like something is there in the back of your mind, nagging away and causing you to be distracted. When you're distracted, it's impossible to focus. Mentally decluttering can help you to clear your mind and allow you to place all your energy and focus on the task you're trying to achieve.

When you use this type of digital detox strategy alongside the time management methods we mentioned in our earlier chapter, you'll find that you complete far more tasks than you did before and you'll feel much better for it.

There is nothing positive about being switched on and contactable all the time. If someone has something urgent to tell you about, they will call you; someone liking your picture on Instagram is not urgent!

Social media can also be very damaging mentally too, especially if you regularly compare yourself to other people as a result of the content you see on the various platforms. There are many benefits to having a detox such as this and although it might seem worrying or even panic-inducing at first, it will get easier as the week goes on. You might even feel like you don't want to use unnecessary sites anymore because you haven't really missed them.

You won't know until you try, and you'll certainly notice that the mental decluttering of not using so much social media and technology is very beneficial for your ability to focus.

Identify And Cut Out Regular Distractions

We've just covered one of the most common distractions around - social media, but there are many other common distractions that are probably running riot in your day and causing your focus and productivity to be seriously off.

This second strategy involves taking a long, hard look at your life and identifying any regular distractions which often clutter up your mind and cause you to be unable to focus on the task you have in front of you.

A few common distractions, aside from social media, are:

- Checking emails too often
- Not drinking enough water or being hungry
- Not being comfortable

- Friends asking you to go for coffee/do something sociable when you need to work or do something else
- Housework, especially if you work from home
- A cluttered working environment
- Unpaid bills
- Worries you haven't addressed
- Health issues

You might have totally different distractions, but these are certainly some of the most common overall. How many of those can you nod along to?

Identifying your personal distraction pitfalls can help you to work to overcome them or simply sidestep them. Let's look at the above list and work out how you can address each one.

- **Checking your emails too often** - We're all guilty of this! Rather than refreshing every few minutes or having push notifications to give your phone a beep every single time you get a piece of spam mail, have two or three dedicated times per day when you check your mail - three if you need emails for work and two if you don't. Perhaps once in the morning and once mid-afternoon is a good option, or once in the morning, once after lunch, and once before you finish work for the day. These set times will take your mind off the wait for the mail and you'll be able to declutter and focus far easier.

- **Being thirsty or hungry** - Not drinking enough water is a huge distraction because it makes your brain feel like mud! Make sure you drink plenty of water throughout the day and if you're feeling hungry, make sure you eat, or at least snack on something healthy. This is a major distraction because you won't be able to think of anything else but the physical feeling and if you don't attend to it, it's going to become all-encompassing and probably quite unhealthy.

- **Not becoming comfortable** - If there a bigger distraction than sitting or standing somewhere very uncomfortable? All you can think about is how uncomfortable you are. So, instead of sticking with it and slogging it out, make yourself comfortable! If you're sitting at a desk and it's not hitting your comfort levels, make some changes. This is one of the easiest distractions to fix, but it could also be that you've become so used to sitting in a certain way or position that you don't even realise you're giving yourself tension or pain! Be mindful of your sitting position and see if changes make a difference.

- **Friends asking you to do something** - If you work from home or you're studying at home, your friends calling around to ask if you want to go for coffee is probably a huge distraction that you really want to give in to. The same goes for when you need to focus on something and you're getting a far better offer. The bottom line is that if you want to focus and get things done, you need to simply forget better options and do it! Turn your phone onto silent so you don't hear it ringing, then check it when you've done what you need to do. If you're busy at home, make sure your friends know that you aren't available that day.

- **Housework, if you work from home** - Another distraction, if you're working or studying from home, is the housework tasks you need to do or the TV. Make a list of what you need to do and plan your day. If you need to do a few chores, make sure you factor those in but have working times when you simply do nothing but the work or study on your list. By giving yourself regular breaks and have times when you do watch TV or do the things which are blocking your mind, you'll find it easier to make progress on both fronts.

- **A cluttered working environment** - We won't dwell on this one because we're going to talk about changing your environment as one of our dedicated strategies. However, it's important to realise that a messy working environment can be a huge focus-blocker. This is because the mess is a mental block and you can't move or focus because of what is around you. If you think back to a time when you had a household clear-out and perhaps decluttered some of your old things, did you feel lighter afterwards? Of course! So the same can be done for your working environment. Get rid of the clutter and notice your focus improving.

- **Unpaid bills** - Money worries can be a huge stress and a major distraction for many. If you have unpaid bills that are causing you to feel mentally blocked and unable to focus, you need to make an action plan and start either paying them off slowly or doing something alternative about them. It's a hard one to deal with, but it's nothing to be ashamed of. Sit down and open those bills, work out how much you owe and how much you have available to pay. If you can pay them, do it. If not, call the people responsible and work out a payment plan. This will take the stress away from your mind, give you back the control and help you regain your focus.

- **Worries you haven't addressed** - Just like unpaid bills, unaddressed worries can be huge focus blockers. They're always there at the back of your mind, nagging away and causing you to feel like you're getting nowhere fast. It's important that you address these things as they're simply going to cause stress over the long-term. Not dealing with issues and pretending they're not happening isn't healthy and it's not going to work out well in the end. In the meantime, you are not going to be able to focus on anything to a high degree. Sit down, write a list of the things you need to address and work through them. If you need support to do this, enlist the help of a friend.

Most worries aren't half as bad as you think they are in reality, so be brave and battle those worries head-on.

- **Heath issues** - An unresolved health issue works in the same way as an unaddressed worry. If you have any health issues that you're concerned about, get it checked out. It could be something that is affecting your focus, such as regular headaches, or it might be something totally unconnected but it is playing on your mind to the point where you can't pay attention to what you're doing. For your own sake and your own health, just head to the doctor and get things checked out; the chances are that it's nothing, but it's better to be safe than sorry.

The good news is that if these are your distractions, you've now got some actionable advice on how to avoid them and fix them. However, if your particular identified distraction is something else, what can you do?

It depends on what the distraction is, but you have to ask yourself whether it's something you need to do something about or something you simply need to avoid. By acknowledging that something is causing you to have a mental focus block, you can take action to reduce its power and therefore ensure you can focus in a better way.

Learn to Invest in Yourself

Low mood and low self-worth can be major problems when it comes to focusing. If you think back to a time when you've been excited about something, perhaps feeling proud of something you've achieved, you'll remember a sense of energy. This gave you purpose and helped you focus on the task at hand.

If you're feeling low, you're not going to have that sense of energy or pride and it can make regular tasks feel like you're trying to swim through mud - you can't see where you're going and you're extremely slow and sluggish, not really making much progress. Most of us can associate with this type of feeling once or twice in our lives, but if you're noticing it on a regular basis, you need to do something about it.

Firstly, if you feel you need to seek help for low mood, then certainly do so. There is no failing in going to your doctor and admitting that you might need a bit of help. That is the strongest thing you can do. However, if you feel like you just need a little cheering up, or you need to boost your sense of self-worth, perhaps after a run of bad luck or poor results, you can do that by investing in yourself.

By this, we mean doing things for you, things which are going to help you achieve your goals and boost your sense of pride in yourself.

For instance, are you always saying 'yes' to other people when you simply don't have the time to do what they've asked of you? It's fine to say 'no'! This is something most of us struggle with, but saying 'no' to something, politely, of course, isn't a failure and it's not going to upset or offend the other person - it's you being honest in your capabilities and refusing to overload yourself. By doing this, you're investing in yourself and your own time.

The bottom line is that most of us don't pay enough attention to our own needs, because we're always paying attention to everyone else's. We assume that by putting ourselves first we're being selfish, but that couldn't be further from the truth! Putting yourself before others occasionally isn't at all selfish, it's something that's necessary. Never underestimate the power of self-care.

We won't dwell too much on this particular technique because a few of the upcoming techniques expand on it a little, such as hobbies and working out what you want in life. However, the biggest piece of actionable advice from this strategy overall is to learn to say 'no' when you either don't have the time to do something, you can't do something, or you simply don't want to do something.

Understand the power of your own time and reinvest that in yourself. Prioritise your downtime in order to do the things you love, such as reading a book, watching your favourite movie, having a hot bath, pampering yourself, spending time with friends, etc. These activities aren't a waste of time simply because they don't achieve anything you can see, because they achieve something far more important - your happiness and your general wellbeing.

How does this help your ability to focus? When you feel happy and healthy within yourself, when your self-worth is at a good level, and your general confidence is high, it's far easier to focus and concentrate, because that 'swimming through mud' feeling isn't there.

Find a New Hobby And Work to be The Best You Can

Do you have hobbies? We're not talking about social media, we're talking about things you do that you enjoy, which get you away from your own mind and which help you to feel good about yourself. How many hobbies that fit that bill do you have?

For many people, if you say to them 'what's your hobby', they'll look at you blankly for a few seconds whilst they try and think of something. If that's you, take it as a sign that you need to come up with a hobby or two which will boost your confidence, give you a greater sense of self-worth, and as a result help you to focus.

There is a competitive streak within all of us, some just have it deeply buried. This strategy is about identifying a new hobby and then working to be the best you can be at that particular endeavour. It can be anything - perhaps you want to be a footballer, a runner, or maybe a top swimmer. Maybe you want to write books, or perhaps you want to make clothes or jewellery. Whatever it is, whether it's something you can win awards in or something you simply enjoy doing, you can do your best to become as good at it as is possible for you.

This helps you to focus because it gives your brain a good workout and increases your motivation levels. You're also doing something you enjoy, which boosts your health and wellbeing and helps you feel happier in general.

Having a new hobby can also increase your social circle, which can give you a great support network when dealing with problems in life. This also gives you a boost of a feel-good factor too.

A little later we're going to talk about brain training exercises, but the point to take from this is that by having a new hobby, you're giving your brain a workout and you're learning something new. This forces new connections in your brain and gets your synapses firing. All of this might sound confusing, but it's the perfect storm in terms of boosting your memory and giving you a boost of focusing ability too.

Most hobbies also teach us something new or something we didn't know before, which again, is great for your brain. The more you challenge yourself and try to do better, improve yourself and be as good at that particular hobby as you possibly can be, you'll notice that your ability to notice small details increases.

If you choose a sporting hobby, you're basically ticking two boxes at once, because you're giving yourself something new to learn about and spend your time on, but you're also getting the exercise we mentioned earlier in our lifestyle chapter.

In terms of avoiding distractions, new hobbies are also a good option. If you're focusing your time and attention on doing something you enjoy, you're not going to be scrolling through social media or spending endless wasted hours in front of the TV. Instead, you're doing something which actually has a meaning and something you're working at improving.

Creative hobbies are ideal for focus because they tend to need close concentration in order to do whatever it is you're trying to do. For instance, if you learn to make clothes, you need to focus on threading the needle seamlessly and quickly, you need to follow a pattern and you need to learn the new techniques for sewing. The same can be said for painting; you'll learn about the different combinations of colours to make new ones, how to hold a paintbrush properly for optimum control, and the different brushstrokes which create the picture you want.

These types of hobbies help to improve your fine motor skills, whilst also occupying your brain and allowing you to develop a hobby which could, in the end, boost your focusing abilities too. If nothing else, you'll enjoy the time and find something which makes you happy!

Identify What is Important to You

Sometimes we simply can't focus because we're not doing the things we want to do. It could also be that your life is going in a direction that isn't really filling you with excitement and joy. When you're in that kind of situation, the ability to concentrate and focus on something carefully is quite difficult.

It's almost like being 'stuck in a rut' in many ways. Every day seems the same, nothing is all that exciting and you're not really filled with a sense of purpose. When you feel this way, being inspired and then finding the ability to focus can be very hard indeed.

Of course, we all go through times like these and sometimes these periods are necessary; if you're working towards something there are going to be transitional periods and times when nothing seems to be moving on the surface, but underneath there is slow progress being made. However, if you're not working towards something, if you simply feel stuck and as though you're just going through the motions every day, your focus is going to take a hit too.

This particular strategy will benefit you on several different levels, not least because it could put you on a completely different path altogether.

Ask yourself whether you're working towards something which is important to you, or if you're doing something which is important to you currently. Sure, we all have to do things we don't want to do occasionally, but that doesn't mean you should be doing this all the time. Your overall purpose in life, the main goal you have, should be a prominent feature.

The first thing to look at is your job, or what you're studying. Does it fill you with enjoyment? Do you find it interesting? Does it inspire you and motivate you? Do you have a long-term plan which incorporates this? If the answer is 'no' to all of the above, you have to take a long, hard look at your life and make some changes.

Of course, you can't make sweeping changes overnight, but you can make a plan to turn your life around if you aren't feeling inspired by the path you're currently on. This will drastically affect your focus because you like what you're doing, you're inspired and motivated by it, and you can see the bigger picture.

One of the biggest focus problems tends to arrive when you are doing a job you don't really like, but you've found yourself in it because it pays the bills and you can do it with your eyes closed, metaphorically speaking. You're in your comfort zone and you're managing to make ends meet every month, so you carry on in that way. You don't realise it at the time, but you're falling deeper and deeper into a rut, which is going to come back and bite you in the future. How can you be truly happy when you're simply clock watching every day, waiting for your salary to hit your bank.

The problem is, far too many people do this. Perhaps you're doing it right now. Surely it's a far better idea to find a job which you truly enjoy most of the time and something which makes you feel like you're doing something worthwhile. That doesn't mean you're never going to have bad days and you're never going to struggle because you're tired, but these days should be few and far between.

So, this technique means you need to sit down and do a life assessment. Are you studying something you enjoy? Are you doing a job you enjoy? Is what you're doing in line with where you see yourself in several years' time? If not, make an action plan to change things, and if it is, try and figure out why you're not feeling inspired more often. It could be that you simply don't get along with your colleagues or you don't like your manager.

When you're doing something that is important to you, you'll find it far easier to focus for longer periods of time, and to greater effect. When you're doing something which you don't really care about, it's far easier to give in to distractions and temptation to do something far more interesting. For instance, if someone says "let's go for coffee" but you've got a report to finish that is boring the socks off you, you're going to say okay to the coffee. However, if you're invested in the report, because it means something to you, it's interesting, or it's going to help you get to where you want to go, you're more likely to dedicate your time to finish it.

It could be that at this point you have no clue what is important to you. It's one of those questions that you know when you're not asked, but when someone puts you on the spot, your mind goes blank. For that reason, don't rush it. Keep a piece of paper with you and scribble down ideas as they enter your brain. Then, after a week or two, sit down and look at that paper and look for recurring themes.

Once you have the information to hand, you can put a plan into place to change your path and therefore, almost miraculously, improve your focus in the most natural of ways.

Remember That Breaks Are Important

Back in our chapter on prioritising and scheduling, we talked about a few different time management techniques; one of those was the Pomodoro Technique. That particular technique is very useful because it incorporates regular breaks into your day, and as a result, you're focused for small periods of time.

The next time you're at work, give this experiment a try; sit down and try and focus on the tasks you have to do for a solid three hours. Don't have a break, don't get up and move around, just sit there and get your tasks done.

Then, try working for half an hour and having a few minutes' break, then working for another half an hour and repeating the breaks.

Which do you think is more productive?

Probably quite surprisingly, it's the method that incorporates regular breaks.

Many studies have shown that long periods of focus are not as productive as short bursts and intervals. The same can be said for exercise in many ways; have you ever heard of HIIT? This stands for High-Intensity Interval Training, and it means that you're exercising at full pelt for a short period of time followed by a break and then repeating. This has been shown to be extremely effective for health and wellbeing, so it makes sense that your brain works in the same way, by using focus and breaks too.

You don't necessarily have to follow the Pomodoro Technique to the letter, you simply need to be mindful of having regular breaks, getting up and walking around, perhaps getting some fresh air, and remembering that sitting at your desk and concentrating constantly for an hour or more at a time is not going to help you get what you need to do, and it's not going to help you focus. If anything it's going to be extremely counterproductive.

Breaks are designed to give your brain a rest. When you focus for more than 25 minutes or so, your brain becomes overloaded. You can't think straight, and you can't come up with new ideas, because you're so bogged down by other stuff you have clogging up your mind! You become tired, you might get a headache, and you begin to notice distractions becoming extremely tempting indeed.

However, when you have regular breaks, you'll find that you can focus much more intensely and get more done, simply because you're allowing your brain the time to recharge. If you head outside into the fresh air on your breaks, and perhaps go for a walk, you're also ensuring that extra blood flow is making its way up to your grey matter. We've already covered why this is beneficial in our chapter on exercise, so it stands to reason that if you're going to have a break, you should do something productive with it, e.g. exercise!

You might be reading this and wondering where the idea of 'pulling an all-nighter' comes from when studying for an upcoming exam or trying to hit a deadline. The truth is that working for long periods of time in that way is not going to benefit you at all. You're going to become slow, sluggish, and your brain is not going to retain information as effectively. However, if you arrange your time so that you're having short bursts of focus, followed by short, recharging breaks, you'll see the differences.

Breaks are necessary for health and wellbeing, not just for focus, but they certainly serve both purposes. Make regular breaks a part of your routine and notice how much more effectively you're able to focus.

Try Mindfulness Meditation

Meditation is not for everyone and it's something you'll need to learn over time and dedicate yourself to, however it is also something which can drastically help you when it comes to your focus.

There are countless different types of meditation out there, but one which has been making waves over the last few years is mindfulness meditation.

The problem is that in the modern-day we tend to either live in the past, regretting the things we didn't do, or lamenting the things we did do, or we live in the future, worrying about things that haven't happened yet, and may never happen at all. All of this creates a picture of unhappiness and can lead to anxiety and depression in the worst cases.

Learning to live in the present day isn't easy, but it's something which, when done, can have major benefits for your health and wellbeing, not least your ability to focus on what you need to do.

Mindfulness is, as we mentioned, living in the present. It means you're less concerned with petty worries, because you're focused on the here and now, and as a result, you're able to enjoy the minute you're in.

For instance, are you someone who sits there with their phone in their hand when they could be talking to a family member or friend? Do you spend time talking to friends who live abroad or people you've never met on social media, and you have a close friend sitting opposite you, who you're totally ignoring in that moment?

Look around the room you're sitting in, if you're out and about, and notice how many people are lost in their phones versus the number of people who are actually conversing, connected to the person they're with, and living in the moment. It's likely to be far more who are simply not present in the moment and instead are stuck in some kind of technological black hole.

Not appreciating the things you have and not appreciating those around you can lead you towards regret in the future, but it can also drastically affect your focus because you're distracted by a million and one different things. When you learn how to be mindful and live firmly in the moment, you'll be able to focus much more effectively, simply because you have fewer things to think about.

People who are well versed in the art of mindfulness are usually far happier than those who aren't. So, how can you begin your mindfulness journey? And, where does meditation comes into it?

Meditation itself takes time to master because you need to be able to cut out the noise around you and focus on silence. This is something most people struggle with, and the first time you try it, you'll probably find you can't do it for long and you end up thinking about the million and one things you have to do on your to-do list. So, instead, we're going to start with a slightly easier exercise.

- Make some time to go outside for a walk, or try this exercise when you're walking to work
- Turn off your phone, or turn it onto silent, so you're not going to be distracted. Resist the urge to put your earphones in and listen to music - you need to be firmly in the moment and the place you're at
- Turn your attention inwards and focus on your breath for a few minutes. Feel your lungs expand as you breathe in slowly through your nose, for a count of five. Hold the breath for a few seconds and then exhale slowly through your mouth in the same manner, noticing your lungs deflating. Repeat this until you feel calm
- When you're ready, notice what is going on around you one thing at a time. For instance,

notice the vibrant green of the grass, the sound of the wind in the trees, the chirping of the birds around you. Really throw yourself into the scene around you and notice the small details.
- If your mind starts to wander and you start to think about other things, simply let the thought flow into your mind and back out again, paying it no serious attention

The more you practice this, the easier it will be to stay in the moment and really notice the small details around you. Don't worry if you don't quite get it the first time; the point is that you're trying.

If you want to take your meditation efforts further, you could also try this particular technique which is known to help with focus.

- Find a quiet time of the day when you're not going to be distracted
- Sit down somewhere comfortable, or lay down if you prefer
- Set your timer for around five to ten minutes, depending on how long you want to meditate for
- Close your eyes and as before, focus on your breath until you feel calm
- As thoughts enter your mind, let them drift back out and don't pay them any firm attention

- When you're ready, bring to mind a task that you need to complete, but you're struggling to do, e.g. you can't really focus on it too well
- Visualise yourself doing that task, focusing and working through the difficult parts. Visualise that you're able to overcome distractions and then visualise how you feel once the task is finally complete
- Hang on to that feeling of pride and success and really examine it. This is the moment you're going to return to when you're actually doing the task, and you run into focus blocks
- Once you're ready, return back to the present moment, focusing on your breath for a few seconds to ground you once more.

The point of that particular meditation is that you're visualising yourself having finished the task that is causing you a problem. You're examining how it feels to overcome those mental blocks you have in place, and you're able to give yourself a point of reference to push you through when you're actually doing the task and struggling.

Again, don't worry if you can't quite connect to the meditation when you first do it. People practice how to meditate for months or even years before they're able to really immerse themselves in a meditative state. All you need to do however is learn how to switch off the noise from outside, which becomes easier the more you do it.

If you're really struggling or if you know you're going to find it difficult to follow your own thoughts, you could also try a guided meditation. You can do this as part of a group, or you can download sample tracks from the Internet. There are also many podcasts that will help you with meditation too.

Meditation has been shown to help improve focus and concentration over time, so the more you practice, the more benefits will come your way.

Set Small Goals on a Daily Basis

When you have something to work towards, it's far easier to stay on track. Your aim helps you to avoid distractions and things that are going to throw your concentration off track, and it helps you to focus far more effectively as a result.

Do you set goals on a daily basis? If not, you need to start.

Most of us have life goals. Some of us don't actually end up achieving them, whilst others do; this is slightly different in that you're going to set small daily goals, things which you can work towards achieving every single day. The more you hit your target, the more your confidence will grow and as a result, you'll find that you're energised and more able to focus on subsequent goals too.

Your goal can be whatever you want it to be, big or small. For instance, you can set a goal to complete your to-do list, which encompasses several different tasks, or you can set a goal to complete the grocery shopping and put it all away. You're basically choosing one particular task or a series of tasks in one lump which are the most important part of your day.

How does this help you to focus? Because the more you reach your goals, the more confident you'll feel, and the more you're giving yourself something solid to work towards. As we've mentioned before, when you have something to aim towards, it's easier to stay on track and you're able to avoid becoming distracted by small things. You're more able to question temptation that comes your way and realise that it's not worth giving in to it, because you won't be able to complete your goal and you like the way it feels when you do.

To set your goal, sit down at the start of every day and work out the most important thing you need to achieve that day. It could be your grocery shopping, as we mentioned before, it could be to go to the gym, or it could be to complete a long report before the end of the day. Choose the thing which is most important to you. Then, write this goal down, or perhaps use an app to track your progress.

Make this goal your priority for the day. Don't put it off or make excuses; make sure that you do everything to work towards it. However, this doesn't mean you should work towards your goal at the detriment of your health - be sensible about it.

Setting small goals helps you to achieve more in the short term and will allow you to see the fruits of your labour. Sometimes when we only focus on long term goals, it can take far too long to actually see any type of progress or success. This can be extremely demotivating because we forget what it's like to achieve something and feel good about it. Part and parcel of success in this way is to be able to feel it, to notice the positivity and the way it pushes you on to achieve more.

By having short term goals that you try your very best to achieve on a daily basis, you're getting a daily drip-feed of that positive energy. This is extremely motivating and your ability to focus will increase as a result.

Try this goal-setting strategy for a week or two and then look back at how it's working for you. Identify whether you're noticing a difference or not.

It's vital to remember that any goal you set for yourself has to be realistic. It's no good setting goals that are going to take a serious stretch to achieve on a daily basis. If you do this, you're setting yourself up for failure and you're going to feel terrible on a rolling basis because nobody has the ability to achieve goals that need a superhuman effort every single day!

Change Your Environment

If you're someone who loves a good clear out, this particular strategy is going to be a great one for you.

Your immediate surroundings have a very strong impact on your ability to focus or otherwise. If you're living or working in a place which is cluttered, full of reminders of painful memories, or it's simply a difficult and uncomfortable place to be in, this is going to cause you to have a serious focus block which makes it almost impossible to get the things done that you want to do.

Physical clutter and mental cutter are two things you need to reduce and cut out, and it can be quite fun doing it. It's certainly a cathartic process and one which will benefit you and other people if you choose to donate certain items to those around you, or to charity.

Let's start with mental decluttering first, as this can be a little more in-depth.

Is there something on your mind?

Be honest. Is there something which is bothering you, annoying you, or causing you to feel that your focus is certainly not what it could be?

- Sit down with a pen and paper at a time when you feel like you're not going to be distracted
- Scribble down anything which comes into your mind that feels significant. It doesn't matter what it is at this point, but if you feel it is more than a simple fleeting thought, scribbling it down
- Keep this paper with you for a day or two and keep adding to it as you come up with ideas
- After a few days, sit down again, but this time you're going to look at your scribblings and try and work out the predominant areas which need a little work. It could be that you have several problems that you aren't quite certain of, or there are certain niggling doubts in your mind that you weren't aware were taking up quite so much of your headspace.

Only when you know what you need to deal with, can you actually get on and do it. There are so many different pieces of information coming our way on a daily basis that we're into information overload. It can be overwhelming, and it can cause you to lose sight of issues that need to be addressed.

Highlight a shortlist of three items you need to deal with first. From there, take the most important or the most pressing and work to resolve it. Then move onto the next, and then the next. Once the first three are sorted out, work on the next three. How long this process goes on for depends upon how many issues you have on your list.

Resolving these issues might be as easy as calling someone and giving them some information, sending an email, or perhaps apologising to someone, but there might be some more time-consuming issues on your list too. In that case, break them down into smaller milestones and work your way through them. You cannot focus on the best of your ability when your mind is full of things you need to work through and deal with.

Some people find it useful to leave a notebook and pen at the side of their bed when they sleep. If you're someone who regularly wakes up and remembers things and then finds it hard to go back to sleep because you're trying not to forget it, simply scribbling it down and forget about it until the morning. Then, when you wake up, you can deal with it however you need to do deal with it, and then forget about it completely.

Mental decluttering isn't as difficult as it sounds, but you do need to be prepared to face challenges head-on if you want to really give yourself a clean slate on which to base your focusing efforts on. You shouldn't expect miracles overnight and you should allow yourself a good amount of time to figure out whatever is clogging up your brain. Don't rush, and give yourself the time to work through everything. When you do that, the results will be far more effective.

You might also find it useful to have someone who you can talk to on a regular basis; this is especially useful if you're someone who bottles things up or doesn't talk about their feelings too often. Let it all out! It feels great and you'll notice that you have less to worry about over time. If that seems too personal, how about starting a journal?

Now we need to focus on physical decluttering.

This is the fun part.

You need to look at any space in which you spend a considerable amount of time. This could be your home, your bedroom, your work, even your car. Whilst it doesn't need to be super-tidy and minimalistic, it does need to be free of clutter and it needs to allow the flow of energy to makes its way through, without being blocked or rerouted elsewhere.

Have you heard of Feng Shui?

Feng Shui is an ancient Chinese practice that uses energy as a way to allow people to feel calm and able to focus as a result. The free flow of energy, or chi, relies upon elements of nature within the space and a total lack of clutter. If you want to really get into this practice in more detail, you also need to have certain elements in different corners or directions. For now, however, we'll just focus on the decluttering side of the coin. This is something you can continue to learn about if you choose to do so.

For every room in your house or every space which you spend a lot of time in, assess it carefully. What don't you need? What don't you use? What do you have in there which is collecting dust and has never been picked up for longer than a few minutes?

This is the ideal time to get rid of old items and perhaps sell them and make a little extra cash, or even better, donate them to charity or gift them to someone in need. Be ruthless, but don't become so obsessed with decluttering that you get rid of things that you do actually need!

The idea is to clear your space down to the minimal items you want and need and then arrange them in a way that allows energy to flow freely. You'll know if this is happening because the space will feel lighter when you walk into it. You won't feel weighed down or heavy when you enter the room and you'll find it far easier to be in that space. As a result, when you're in there and you're trying to focus on a task, it will become far easier for you to pay attention and get done, what needs to be done.

Of course, once you've decluttered you need to make sure that your space remains clear and free of new clutter. Be mindful of anything that you buy and make sure that you don't simply replace the items you've got rid of with new things. Whilst you don't need to develop a minimalist mindset, you do need to be wary of what you're buying so you're not basically undoing your good work!

Give the mental decluttering a go first and then work on your physical space. The physical side of it is far easier than the mental, but both will give you a much better foundation on which to build your increased focusing efforts.

A cluttered desk does not equal a genius; it equals someone who cannot find the piece of paper they put down, someone who can't remember where they left their pen, and it equals someone who can't possibly focus in the best way. Don't listen to these old adages that tell you working in mess signals creativity; if you compare the process of working in a tidy and streamlined environment versus working in a totally cluttered and messy one, you'll see the differences immediately!

Avoid Multi-Tasking at All Costs

If there is one focus damaging habit you can have, it's multi-tasking.

You might think that doing several tasks at once makes you a productive whizz, but how many tasks are you actually completing? It's more likely that you're doing little bits of tasks but never really getting anything done.

You see, your brain cannot focus on several different tasks to a high degree. If you want to do something properly, focus on it, do it, pat yourself on the back, and then move on to the next item on your priority list. Do not attempt to multi-task if you want to make progress!

It's single-tasking all the way or not at all if you want to increase your focus to the point where you're able to get things done and not allow your motivation to be affected.

Let's explain why this is the case with an example.

Let's say that you have a report to finish, which is currently half done, you need up upload some articles that were written the week before. Again, these are just random examples of tasks; this advice pertains to any task, whether home, work or anything else.

If you attempt to finish writing the report whilst uploading at the same time, you might think that you're literally 'killing two birds with one stone'; however when you delve a little deeper you'll find that both tasks are taking you longer than they would if you focused on one solely. You're also more likely to make mistakes, because you're not giving a single task your total focus and concentration, and your brain is half on one and half on the other.

It's likely trying to concentrate in a room full of screaming and crying children. It's impossible. Your brain will focus for a while, it will hang on, hang on, and you'll feel it slipping away before boom! You've read the same sentence three times over and your focus has completely upped and left the building. After that, attempting to get back on the horse is pointless until everything calms down and you've also managed to destress yourself from the entire situation.

Multi-tasking is the same because it's like you're stretching your brain too thin. When that happens, you can't possibly complete anything to the best of your ability because you're not completely focusing on one thing.

Surely it's better to give one task your total focus and then move on to the next?

The problem is that we're all so stretched for time that the temptation to try and do two tasks at the same time as one can be irresistible. You have to remind yourself that it's a fallacy and simply doesn't work. It's a better option to use time management techniques, such as the Pomodoro Technique or time challenges if you want to do more and be productive. At least these techniques allow you to make actual progress, whereas multi-tasking is simply fake progress, which in the end will leave you more stressed out than you were before!

The actionable point to take away from this strategy is to focus on a task, do it, complete it and then move on to the next. Avoid falling foul of the multi-tasking fallacy and learn to focus your mind on just one thing completely.

Use Brain Training Exercises

Use it or you lose it. That's basically what your brainpower comes down to.

The ageing process can, in some ways, reduce your brain power and effectiveness, so it's important to keep giving your brain a workout on a regular basis. It's a little like trying to tone your muscles at the gym; you need to keep flexing them and exercising them so they become stronger over time. When you do this, you can rely upon those muscles to keep you strong and healthy. Your brain is the same.

Brain training exercises came to prominence a few decades ago, and they're also very useful for helping you to learn how to focus in a more detailed way. You don't have to learn how to do sudoku (almost impossible) in order to give your brain a workout, and there are a few fun exercises you can try instead. Let's look at a few you might like to try.

- **Jigsaw puzzles** - Studies have shown that doing jigsaw puzzles can help to boost your brain's abilities and can also help to protect you against degenerative ageing. You'll also be focusing on the pieces and where they fit; focusing is like a muscle too, the more you use it, the easier and stronger it becomes.
- **Playing cards** - There are countless card games you can try and you can also enlist the help of a friend to give it a social edge! Try solitaire (the computer game is just as effective), poker, bridge, or gin rummy as a few useful games that will get your brain firing into action.
- **Learn to play a musical instrument** - Studies have shown that learning to play a new instrument can help to form new brain connections and therefore help you to focus more effectively over time. It's

also a great hobby to have, and we mentioned earlier about how hobbies can help to boost your focus skills, whilst boosting your confidence at the same time.

- **Try matching games** - Download a game onto your phone which uncovers cards and then covers them over, whilst you have to remember them and match them once more. This can help to boost your memory, and any type of memory training can also help with your general focus.
- **Word searches** - A puzzle book or app will do the trick here! Word searches are one of the oldest ways to keep your brain healthy and they're ideal for boosting your focus and giving your brain a general workout.

Learning something new is also a great way to give your brain a cognitive workout because you're building new connections and firing those brain synapses on a more regular basis. When you do this, you become more alert, and you guessed it, more focused too.

So, what do you want to learn? Perhaps you want to learn a language, a musical instrument, or maybe you just want to learn a little new general knowledge. Whatever it is, get started today!

Points to Take From This Chapter

The ten strategies we've talked about over the course of this final chapter are perfect for naturally boosting your focus levels. However, you shouldn't forget the other methods we have talked about previously in the book, such as time management, health and wellbeing, etc. When you combine all of this together, you create the perfect storm, a way of firing your focus into line and allowing you to do far more in the time you have.

It's important to remember that there is no one size fits all answer here, so it could be that not all of these strategies work for you; try them all out and then focus on the ones which help you the most. By doing this, you'll identify the go-to methods you can use time and time again.

The main points to take from this chapter are:

- Learning different strategies to improve your focus takes time
- You might not find use in all the strategies, but you will find use in many if you attempt them all
- Using your brain on a regular basis, e.g. learning something new, will allow you to strengthen your cognitive function and create a stronger foundation on which to build

- Time management is also a very useful way to learn how to focus in a better way
- Make sure you get enough sleep, eat a healthy diet and exercise regularly in addition to the focus boosting strategies in this chapter.

Conclusion

And there we have it! We've come to the end of our book and by now you should be feeling quite uplifted and optimistic about your chances of boosting your focus and, as a result, learning to do more with your time.

We all have the ability to focus within it, however, certain situations, problems, and issues can affect the amount of focus we have from one moment to the next. It might be that just one task causes you a particular problem, simply because you don't like it, or it might be that you can't focus on anything because you're tired and you're not placing importance upon your sleep routine.

Focus basically dictates whether or not you complete anything. It dictates how well you do things and how much you do. If you can't focus, everything will go wrong. Focus isn't just accuracy, it's productivity in its most basic form.

The information and strategies we've covered in this book have given you a fantastic starting point on which to grow. Remember to take your time and don't rush through it; if you want to improve your focus you need to allow yourself the room to complete the task.

Whether you want to pay more attention to work, school, study in general, learning new things, or anything else, you need to understand the basics. Looking after your general health is where you should start - feed your brain the things it wants and needs, make sure you're getting enough sleep, and exercise on a regular basis. If you don't do the basics, you won't see any progress or success with other strategies.

As with any self-development niche, learning to become more focused is something you will never regret and it will never be something you waste your time on.

Your journey starts today!

A Short message from the Author:

Hey, did you enjoy reading this book? I'd love to hear your thoughts!

Many readers do not know how hard reviews are to come by, and how much they help a new author like myself. Reviews alone are what typically makes my book stand out in the crowd and persuades another person to choose this book.

I would be incredibly grateful if you could take just 60 seconds is all it takes to write a brief review (even if it's just a few sentences) on whatever bookstore or marketplace you purchased this book from!

Thank you for taking the time to share your thoughts!

More from Jean-Claude Leveque

-Conquer your Emotions
-Conquer your Motivation
-Conquer your Purpose
-F*ck Anxiety
-F*ck Panic Attacks

www.ingramcontent.com/pod-product-compliance
Lightning Source LLC
Chambersburg PA
CBHW021439080526
44588CB00009B/606